THE BEST OF
AMERICA

Text by
Edward Tosques

Photographs by
Andrea Pistolesi

BONECHI

THE ON-THE-ROAD MYTH

America's most immediate feature has always been its sweeping spatial vistas, the vertical ones of its skyscrapers and the horizontal ones of its open countryside, its prairies, forests and deserts, those transmitter-spires or gray ribbons of highway stretching away, up to the clouds or off to the horizon, tending so far as to turn into a kind of transcendence, a reality of such a sheer and grandiose physicality as to become the metaphysical symbol of the individual's infinite freedom, his cutting loose from all social and personal ties. Quest or escape, or a little of both. It was like that already for the pioneers, who were always seeking a better life somewhere ahead, *while also fleeing from something* behind; *in rare cases, such as that of the Mormons, from real persecution, but most often just from some ordinary failure or scandal - bankruptcy, marital disaster, trouble with the law - something the lure of the open frontier gave them an irresistible temptation not to confront. Thus an ambiguous act of mixed evasion or, worse, cowardice in terms of what they were leaving behind, and fortitude and heroism in terms of what lay ahead. The American myth of individual freedom grew out of this inbetween state, this freewheeling indeterminacy or suspension, unthinkable in most other cultures and eras, which as a rule have been marked by a static destiny. The gesture of pulling up and moving on, as the prelude to starting over again, repeated and repeated as long as one's energies lasted and there was still frontier to flee to, with time became an end in itself. Pure motion lost its scope and became an existential purpose, the quest its own objective, the very poetry of being. It is a myth which in our time has been immortalized in so much popular American art, from Kerouac's novel* On the Road *(which lent its name to the whole genre), to the innumerable westerns and gangster movies, to films like* Easy Rider *and* Thelma and Louise *or their stylized European-conceived counterparts, Antonioni's* Zabriskie Point *and Wenders'* Paris, Texas; *and to songs like "Bobby McGee", whose haunting refrain, "Freedom's just another word for nothing left to lose", expresses it all.*

THE BEST OF AMERICA
Project and editorial conception: Casa Editrice Bonechi
Picture research: Monica Bonechi
Graphic design and make-up: Manuela Ranfagni
Editing: Anna Baldini
Text by Edward Tosques
Map by Studio Grafico Bellandi & Mariani - Pistoia - Italy

© Copyright 1996 by Casa Editrice Bonechi - Firenze - Italy

Photographs from the archives of Casa Editrice Bonechi taken by Andrea Pistolesi.

Photographs from the archives of Realy Easy Star: p. 60 above (I. Bolondi); *p. 18, 25* (S. Fournier); *p. 60 center and below, 98, 99, 100, 152 above, 153* (G. Furghieri); *p. 149 center* (M. Maniaci); *p. 112, 113, 149 below* (S. Montanari); *p. 62, 149 above* (L. Pranovi); *p. 19 above* (C. Rizzi); *p. 101* (P. P. Viola); *p. 152 below* (C. A. Zabert). *Photographs from the archives of K & B News: p. 19 below* (A. Biancalani); *p. 61, 63* (G. Persichino).

p. 142: Photograph by S. Cellai; *p. 117: Photograph by* K. Glaser; *p. 59: Photograph by* K. Wang; *p. 144, 145:* © The Walt Disney Company.
The Publisher thanks the Walt Disney Company *for the kind cooperation.*

ISBN 88-8029 - 379 - 6

* * *

Yet it is wrong to think that America's sweeping vistas serve only as a flat backdrop against which to move in an eternal present with no temporal depth. The time-dimension counts too in America, in the end just as much as the space-dimension, and just as much as it does in exploring the archeological stratifications of Europe or any other part of the Old World. In point of fact, there are several kinds of time in America, running parallel to each other, and often intersecting; four of them to be precise.

THE GEOLOGICAL PAST

There is first the titanic pre-human antiquity of geological time. This is felt in America as in few other areas on earth, above all in places like the Mesas and the Canyonlands of the West, or Yellowstone Park, or the Tetons (with its odd assonance with Titans). There, such technical terms as tectonic movement, uplifting, erosion and hydrothermal activity acquire downright mystic significations beside the wonders which they describe and which are visible to all. Wonders which duly dwarf mankind with their pre- and (probably) post-human, inexorably slow metamorphoses, revelations of Nature's divinity, what the Indians call the "Great Spirit". Photographers like Ansel Adams have devoted their lives to capturing this aspect of America, in images that have the abstract intricacy and epic force of great symphonic music.

Meteor crater, Arizona, marks the spot where a 60,000-ton meteor crashed to earth some 49,000 years ago.

THE PAST OF THE NATIVE-AMERICAN CULTURES

Second, there is the living or just recently expired human past of the Native American civilizations. These include the Pueblos of Arizona and New Mexico, which once constituted the northern rim of the vast Aztec Empire, as well as the tenaciously preserved traditions of tribes all over the present-day North- and Southwest and the Great Plains, from the Nez Percé to the Navajo and the Sioux. In its differing American time-scheme, this antiquity corresponds to Europe's pre-Homeric and to Asia's pre-Mesopotamian ancestors, that is to say, to the Neolithic and Paleolithic ages of five to four-hundred millennia ago, during the late Pliocene and the whole Pleistocene epoch. In the Old World, traces of this long early age of mankind have been all but obliterated by the layers upon layers of anthropologically more "advanced" civilizations that followed. When lions, tigers and elephants roamed over Europe and the Middle East, these peoples hunted and gathered in rudimentary encampments. They may have been "primitive", yet we owe to them the development of language as we know it, and religion, and art, and the first scientific observations of things. Archeological evidence shows that their cultures were very similar to those of Native Americans before and even long after the arrival of the white man. Therefore Americans, and through them the rest of mankind, are privileged in being able to recuperate this Native American heritage, and above all what is still intact and alive in it, discovering the deep vital roots of an exceptionally ancient humanity, roots which are more than ever precious to us in a world devastated by "progress".

THE MYTHIC-HISTORIC PAST OF EUROPEAN EXPLORATION AND SETTLEMENT

Third, there is the antiquity of Europe's settlement of America. This spans a mere five-hundred years, if we take as our outside starting date Columbus's landing in Santo Domingo, and less than four-hundred years if we count from the Pilgrims' landing at Plymouth Rock - practically yesterday, from the standpoint of European history. But here again, the American time-scheme works differently, and what in Europe counts as relative modernity, in America gets stretched into the remoteness of myth. The primitive struggle for survival, the slow taming of an immense wilderness, the forging of a nation, the conflicts over slavery and the abuse of the Indians, the successive migrations westward. It is history of an antiquity analogous to that of the Bible or the Homeric epics, which makes an American feel those four or five centuries as something vastly longer and more embedded in the mists of legend than a European does his. Thus cities like Saint Augustine, Boston or Philadelphia seem positively Sumerian, while New York's turn-of-the-century tenements are akin to the medieval quarters of Paris or Prague, and the Empire State Building corresponds to the Palace of Versailles.

THE KALEIDOSCOPIC PASTS OF AMERICA'S MELTING POT

America's fourth and final temporal dimension lies in the melting-pot phenomenon. As everyone knows, America is an amalgam of every culture in the world, each with its own language and customs. On the surface these differing cultures seem to vanish as the successive generations of native-born assimilate into the single dominant mainstream.

Thus a young Black from Alabama whose ancestors came over on the slave ships, a young Chicano from California whose ancestors were Pueblo Indians or Spanish colonists, a young Italian-American from New York whose ancestors were dirt-poor Sicilian peasants, and a young Wasp from Indiana whose ancestors were Scottish tradesmen, are under their skins indistinguishable from each other. Which is of course true. But at the same time the cultures of their origins go on surviving deep within them, even if in fragmented form, by way of a hundred family and ethnic rituals - a few phrases of dialect, a few down-home dishes, a few old photos or other keepsakes, and a few mental or behavioral tics perhaps barely perceivable to an outsider.

3

America's swiftly-moving mainstream, rather than extinguish these traits and customs, precisely by its superficial slickness and its indifference to their existence, paradoxically preserves them as under amber. Nothing of the sort would be possible in their countries of origin where these traits and customs would be - indeed, have been - swept into a constant process of interaction and change. In this way, linguistic forms or folk beliefs of families that migrated to America 100 or more years ago have perfectly retained their archaic character, while back home they have been radically modernized. This duality of the melting pot has the effect of creating pockets of antiquity in the very heartland of America, in settings where one would least expect to find them: not so much among the recently arrived Russian or Chinese immigrants as among their thoroughly assimilated cousins in hypermodern, middle-class suburbia. Occasionally this time-warp effect is intentional, as among the Amish of Pennsylvania, but usually it is just accidental, as in the peculiar way Brooklyn's Williamsburg section breathes the flavor of old Warsaw, and Manhattan's Little Italy breathes the flavor of old Naples, and a good ethnic restaurant in Detroit recreates the magic of Canton or Cairo better than many a voyage to these same places.

Canyon de Chelly National Monument, Arizona, whose shaping has spanned many millennia.

A BRIEF HUMAN HISTORY OF AMERICA

But a just appreciation of the monuments and settings depicted in this book requires at least a brief review of America's *human* past, which can be broken down into its two great phases of human presence, the Native-American cultures and the age of European (and extra-European) exploration, settlement and immigration.

THE NATIVE-AMERICAN CULTURES

In 1492, Columbus called the natives he encountered on the island of Hispaniola Indios because he believed he had touched ground in the East Indies. The misnomer stuck, and to this day we call "Indians" the millions of Native Americans scattered all over North and South America in some 2,000 distinct cultures.

Native American history is generally divided into **pre-Columbian**, the period prior to the arrival of Europeans in America, and **post-Columbian**, the period subsequent to their arrival. Although the Indians of North America became subject to white domination much later than the Indians of Mexico and Peru, they were conditioned by the Europeans early on, in the northeast through the fur-trade and in the Great Plains region by the introduction of the horse.

THE PRE-COLUMBIAN ERA

The original Indian settlers arrived tens of thousands of years ago from southeast Asia, probably across the still frozen Bering Straits at the end of the last Ice Age. These paleo-Indians gradually spread out over the North and South American continents, discovering bountiful environments full of edible plants and large and small game. But with the passage of the centuries many game species became extinct or less plentiful, and Indian tribes had to adapt to local, mainly vegetable, food resources, and to develop food-processing tools.

Before the Europeans came, most Indian tribes inhabiting what is now the United States consisted of small bands (20-50 people) of nomadic foragers, though some larger tribes, numbering 1,000 or more, practiced a rudimentary form of agriculture and lived in semi-permanent villages. Only the Pueblo Indians of the Southwest, occupying the northernmost rim of the great Aztec civilization, used the more sophisticated farming techniques of fertilization, terracing and irrigation, which enabled them, through the yield of surpluses, to build commercial networks of roads and towns.

The Indians living in the western coastal areas were mainly fishers, such as the Tungit and the Kwakiutl, or foragers, such as the Nez Percé, the Yakima, the Modoc and the Chumash. The Great Plains Indians, such as the Cheyenne, the Sioux and the Apaches, were hunters of bison. The Indians of the eastern woodlands, the Iroquois and the Algonquin groups, were builders of earthwork mounds and walled towns with as many as 30,000 inhabi-

Sitting Bull, legendary Sioux Chief, who defeated Custer at the Little Big Horn.

tants. In the southeast tribes such as the Cherokee, the Natchez and the Seminoles, with their populous, palisaded villages and temple structures, realized the highest cultural development north of the Aztec civilization, by which they were deeply influenced. The Southwest cultivators, such as the Mojave and the Pueblo peoples, and the foragers, such as the Apaches, lived in the Arizona-New Mexico area, the Pueblo Indians in particular inhabiting villages of multistory apartment dwellings.

THE POST-COLUMBIAN ERA

Contact with the European (and later white American) settlers sooner or later devastated the ways of life, and in some cases the very survival, of the Indian peoples. Although the policy of the early English settlers, and of the U.S. government up to the 1870s, was to consider the Indian tribes as sovereign nations with whom they negotiated to purchase land, the Indians did not comprehend the concept of land ownership and believed they were merely selling usage rights; thus conflicts inevitably ensued. Further, the countless treaties the U.S. government signed with the various tribes were constantly being broken by the waves of land-hungry settlers. The tribes of the Pacific northwest, already decimated by disease, firearms and alcohol by the mid-18th-century, managed at least to remain on their homelands. The California Indians, on the other hand, were virtually exterminated by the Spaniards and later by the hordes of prospectors during the 1849 Gold Rush. In the Great Plains the bison, the Indians' food staple, were wantonly slaughtered by the westward-moving pioneers and the tribes brutally forced onto reservations. The Indian peoples of the Atlantic seaboard were all decimated by war and disease in the earliest days of European settlement, and the survivors forced to relocate to the Oklahoma Territory in the early 19th century. The Southwest Indians were, with intermittent resistance, subdued and partially integrated by the Spaniards, except for the Apaches who were defeated by the U.S. Army in the 1840s. The Navajo-Apaches today make up the largest Native-American group, and, along with the Hopi, have best preserved their traditional cultures.

The material contributions of Native-American cultures are many and significant: tobacco, rubber, a new kind of cotton, medicinal plants, turkeys, toboggans, moccasins, snowshoes, plus the cultivation of maize, beans, potatos, manioc, tomatoes, chili peppers, cacao, pineapples, squashes, artichokes, cashews, and maple sugar. Their spiritual contribution could also have been very great had

Tombstone, Arizona, a history book of the Wild West;
Toppenish, Washington, mural depicting an Indian
camp.

they possessed a level of technology that would have obliged Europeans to respect them. But, apart from a few insightful souls in every age, the attitude of most whites was, as a rule, one of contempt, brutality and systematic ignorance of Indian cultures. However, since the 1970s Indians in the U.S. have been playing a more actiive role in determining their destinies. The Bureau of Indian Affairs, now largely staffed by Indians, is setting more ambitious goals of higher education, employment, and the revival of traditional Indian lore. And American society is in some measure reevaluating the past and trying to make up for it.

EUROPEAN SETTLEMENT
The great age of European exploration began with the first voyage of Christopher Columbus in 1492. During the 150 years that followed, Spain, France, England and Portugal explored and traded in the New World. The Spanish claimed Florida, Mexico, and the region west of the Mississippi River; the French settled Canada; and the English colonized the region along the Atlantic coast.

BRITISH COLONIES IN NORTH AMERICA
England began its colonization of North America in the economically and intellectually bustling Elizabethan era, basing its claims on the 1497-99 voyages of John Cabot. After the abortive Roanoke, Virginia colony of the 1580s, the British, under the auspices of the London Company, established Jamestown in 1607. After a period of severe hardships Jamestown prospered with the tobacco trade. The labor force was composed primarily of indentured servants, and the Chesapeake Bay area offered a great opportunity for poor English people. In 1632 the Roman

Catholic Maryland colony was established. In 1620 Puritan Separatists (the Pilgrims) landed on the Mayflower at Plymouth Rock. They established Plymouth Colony. In 1629 the Massachusetts Bay Company organized a settlement around Boston. There followed a great Puritan Migration (1629-42). Baptists founded Rhode Island (1644); Puritans established Connecticut in 1644; and the New Hampshire settlement was chartered as a royal colony in 1679. After Cromwell's Commonwealth era, the newly restored crown founded Carolina (1663) and wrested New Netherland from the Dutch, renaming the area New York and New Jersey. There followed the Quaker colonies of Pennsylvania (1681) and Delaware (1682). Fighting with the diseased and poverty-stricken Indians of the New England area broke out in 1675-76 in the bloody King Philip's War. Meanwhile, the Five Nations of the Iroquois League maintained power over the vast region from New York west to Lake Superior. The French and Indian Wars (1754-63), in which certain Indian tribes sided with the British and others with the French, culminated in the British takeover of Canada and France's fur-trading Ohio Valley region.

SOCIAL AND ECONOMIC TRENDS IN 18TH-CENTURY AMERICA
Throughout the 18th century the British colonies in America prospered, became refined, and grew from the scant 250,000 population of 1700 to 5,300,000 by 1800. Many non-English settlers, such as Germans and Scots-Irish, poured in, as well as convicts from English debtors' prisons, some of whom founded Georgia colony.
From 1619 slaves from Africa began to be imported into the colonies, first by the Dutch and later directly by the English, and by the latter half of the 18th century their numbers in many areas equalled or surpassed those of whites. This abundant slave labor made possible the growth of the great indigo, rice and cotton plantations of the south. Religious trends during the 18th century alternated between an Enlightenment-inspired deism and various revivalist movements culminating in the "Great Awakening" fostered by the Methodist preachers John Wesley and George Whitefield.

THE AMERICAN REVOLUTION
The victory over France in the French and Indian Wars made the colonists exult with pride and with a new specifically American identity. At the same time, England was left with an immense war debt which it tried to meet by imposing a new tax, the Stamp Act, on all printed documents. But upon strenuous protest by the Colonials this tax was repealed. New tension then arose because the standing army the British maintained along the western frontier inhibited settlement of the vast newly-annexed territories. Colonial distrust of England grew, and the English responded by imposing new taxes to support their army and governing commissioners, as well as new restrictions on political freedom. Mob attacks against revenue commissioners provoked the Boston Massacre of 1770, and in 1773 colonials staged the Boston Tea Party. Meanwhile, Samuel Adams roused anti-British sentiment among the colonies, and in 1774 the first Continental Congress took place in Philadelphia.
The War for Independence offically began in 1775 with the Battles of Lexington and Concord. The Colonial militias, though small, ill-equipped and scattered throughout the colonies, enjoyed the advantages of the immense wilderness and the aid of England's enemies - France in the lead - who kept England engaged in conflicts from the Caribbean to India. In 1776 the Continental Congress

issued the Declaration of Independence, and General Washington reversed colonial defeats with his victory at the Battle of Trenton. The decisive event was the Yorktown Campaign of 1781, in which American forces with the help of the French defeated the English under Lord Cornwallis.

THE NEW NATION TAKES SHAPE

The American Colonies officially became the United States of America with the ratification of the Articles of Confederation in 1781. The Confederation Congress, however, was too limited in its powers to govern effectively, and after a period of financial and political instability, state leaders called a new Constitutional Convention in 1787. Using the English parliamentary system as a model, the Constitutional Convention established a popularly elected national Congress, an elected President, a Supreme Court, and a Constitution. However, the North and the South soon differed as to how the country should be run. The North, represented by Alexander Hamilton, favored an authoritative Federal Government that would finance and regulate commerce and industry, while the South, represented by Thomas Jefferson, favored states' rights and laissez-faire. John Adams, the nation's second president, implemented Federalist policies, while the next president, Thomas Jefferson, worked to counteract Federalism. Jefferson's most dramatic contribution though was the Louisiana Purchase (1803), which overnight more than doubled the size of the United States, extending it to the base of the Rockies. Meanwhile, the young Republic got caught in the midst of conflicts between England and revolutionary France. Its being forced to submit to British confiscation of American ship cargoes and to the impressing of American sailors into the British navy led to the War of 1812, from which America once again emerged victorious thanks to the help of the French.

AN ERA OF ECONOMIC AND TERRITORIAL EXPANSION, AND OF "GOOD FEELING"

From 1815 to 1850 the American economy enjoyed unceasing growth. The cotton boom financed the flowering of the Deep South; the Erie Canal stimulated agricultural settlement of the Ohio River Valley; practically all Indians east of the Mississippi were placed on reservations or forced to move to the Great Plains west of the Missouri River; canals and railroads penetrated further and further west; new states came into being about every 2 1/2 years; and the great midwestern cities, such as Chicago, were born. In the North the factory system developed, and the enormous capital from the Gold Rush financed the wildest business schemes as well as swift settlement of the western territories. A second Great Awakening, originating in New England, led to a ferment of social reform, most notably to the movement for the abolition of slavery. The period 1815-60 saw the U.S. boundaries stretch practically to their present-day limits. In 1818 the 49th parallel was fixed as the U.S.-Canada border up to the Rockies, and in 1819 Spain ceded Florida and the Oregon Country. In the 1840s the thirst for continent-wide expansion found official expression in the theory of Manifest Destiny. This ideological rationale justified first the annexation of Texas in 1845, and then the Mexican War (1846-48) which brought about the annexation of New Mexico and Alta California and the establishment of the Rio Grande as the nation's southern boundary. In 1846 the 49th-parallel boundary was stretched to the Pacific, and in 1853 the U.S. purchased the southern areas of New Mexico and Arizona. By 1860 the Union included 33 states,

Jerome, Arizona, a famous mining town of the Old West; Natchez, Mississippi: Stanton Hall, a typical "manse" of the Old South.

and the population had expanded from the 9.6 million of 1820 to 31.5 million. The period 1817-1829, known as the Era of Good Feeling, saw the construction of roads and bridges through the interior, the primacy of the Supreme Court in questions regarding interstate and international commerce and slavery (which it prohibited in most of the new territories), as well as the formulation of the Monroe Doctrine, which proclaimed U.S. predominance in the Western Hemisphere. Meanwhile, the old division between Hamiltonian Federalists and Jeffersonian Republican-Democrats continued in the formation of the Whig (pro-strong central government) and Democratic (pro-laissez-faire) political parties.

THE SLAVERY QUESTION

In the 1840s-50s the slavery question gained prominence, partly through the Abolitionist movement, and partly through the fear of most northerners that the competition of slavery would eventually destroy the free-labor system. With the opening up of the western frontier the sectional contrasts between North and South worsened beyond all possibility of compromise, for each insisted on exporting its social and economic ways of life into the new territories. When, with the connivance of a pro-Southern U.S. Supreme Court, slavery was approved by popular sovereignty in the Kansas-Nebraska territory (1854), the anti-Southern Republican Party was born in the North. Anti-Southern sentiment increased still further by the Supreme Court's decision in the Dred Scott case (1857), which gave slave-owners the right to reappropriate runaway slaves who fled to the North. In 1860 the Republican candidate, Abraham Lincoln, was elected President.

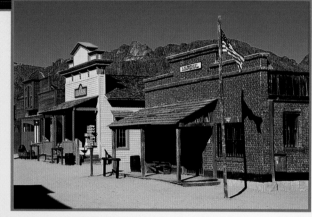

Toppenish, Washington: one of the places seeing a rebirth of Indian cultures; Old Tucson, Arizona, a precise reconstruction of an Old West town.

THE WAR BETWEEN THE STATES

As soon as Lincoln was elected, South Carolina seceded from the Union, and Mississippi, Florida, Alabama, Georgia and Louisiana followed suit. Their representatives met to form the Confederate States of America. The Civil War began officially with the Confederate bombardment of Fort Sumter in 1861. Then Virginia, Arkansas, North Carolina and Tennessee seceded, and the Confederate capital was established at Richmond, Va. Four years of bloody, indecisive fighting followed, with a staggering death toll: 620,000, more than the total U.S. losses in World War II. While the North had the advantages of a much larger population and a well-developed industrial and railway system, the South had only to defend its borders and possessed a greater will to fight and abler military leaders. In 1863 Lincoln issued the Emancipation Proclamation, freeing slaves in all the rebel states. He enforced an economic blockade of the South, and eventually managed to cut the Confederacy in half by taking control of the Mississippi River. The decisive event of the war was the smashing of a Confederate offensive at the Battle of Gettysburg in 1863. There followed Grant's capture of Richmond and Sherman's harrowing drive through the South down to Georgia and up through the Carolinas. In 1865 Gen. Robert E. Lee surrendered to Grant at Appomatox, and the war was over.

THE POST-CIVIL WAR PERIOD

The Republican administration of the victorious Union immediately implemented strong central government action, such as aid to capitalists to construct the railroads and exploit natural resources in the new territories, plus the establishment of free land grants to settlers. Lincoln's ambitious Reconstruction Program was aborted by his assassination right at the war's end. His successor Andrew Johnson even sought to restore a milder form of slavery, though the Republican-dominated Congress reacted by drafting the 14th Amendment, which guaranteed equal civil rights to all U.S. citizens, and by establishing military governments throughout the South to insure free elections. However, practically nothing was done to improve the social and economic conditions of the former Black slaves. After some initial cooperation by the South in Reconstruction, distrust grew that the Republican government was exploiting its power to favor corrupt capitalist speculators (called "carpet-baggers").

Organizations like the Ku Klux Klan were born to restore white supremacy, and by 1876 the Federal government had left the race question wholly in the hands of the South, which promptly set about establishing the Jim Crow laws. This body of legislation, institutionalizing racial segregation, was upheld by the Supreme Court in an 1896 decision. Black leaders disagreed on how to react: Booker T. Washington felt that Blacks should not demand equality, but be content with exercising crafts professions to prove their abilities to whites, while W.E.B. Du Bois urged uncompromising protest in favor of thorough social integration.

THE GILDED AGE

There followed (1870s-1890s) the Gilded Age, a period which favored individualism and capitalist expansion at the expense of the poor and the socially outcast. Industry grew at a rapid pace. In 1869 the Transcontinental Railroad was completed, and by 1890 the U.S. possessed 1/3 of the world's entire railroad trackage. The Indians were brutally exterminated or forced to live on reservations, and from the 1860s large-scale cattle ranching and agriculture invaded the Great Plains.

THE SECOND GREAT WAVE OF IMMIGRATION, AND THE PROCESS OF URBANIZATION

In the period 1860-1890 the U.S. population redoubled to number 63 million, largely through the influx of immigrants from southern and eastern Europe. This great new wave of immigration continued through the first decade of the new century. Most of these fresh arrivals settled in the cities, whose populations swelled, and a contrast grew up between the predominantly Catholic-Jewish urban areas and the predominantly Protestant rural areas. The labor movement began, first with the Knights of Labor (1878) and later with the American Federation of Labor, both of which promoted sweeping social and economic reforms. The Great Depression of the 1890s further stressed the contrast between ethnic urban centers and the "wasp" rural areas, for the latter favored inflation (the Populist Party's "free silver" platform) so as to raise agricultural prices, while the former favored Republican policies of government intervention to keep prices down. The battle ended with a Republican victory and its domination of U.S. politics through the 1920s.

TOWARD BECOMING A WORLD POWER

In the 1890-1920 period there was a resurgence of U.S. expansionism under the guise of progressivist ideals that proposed spreading the "American Way of Life" throughout the Western Hemisphere and the rest of the globe - the U.S.'s first gropings toward becoming a world power. U.S. interventions in Latin America culminated in the Spanish-American War (1898), through which the U.S. assumed Cuba, Puerto Rico, Guam and the Philippines as protectorates. Later the Hawaiian Islands were also annexed. Theodore Roosevelt undertook the construction of the Panama Canal (1903), extending the Monroe Doctrine to include occupation of Panamanian territory. With these additions (plus the purchase of the Alaska Territory from Russia back in 1867), the U.S. borders spread well beyond the North American continent.

Chicago: these sculptures by Mirò and Picasso symbolize America's forefront role in the era of modernity; New York, Brooklyn Bridge.

THE ROARING 20s

The 1920s were a period of isolationism and prosperity, and of a focus on private concerns. It was the age of the airplane and of the mass diffusion of the automobile, the radio, and motion pictures, which drastically transformed American society into the quick-paced, hedonistic, urban-oriented quintessence of modernity. Women made a great leap toward social emancipation, and the 19th Amendment (1920) granted them the right to vote. However, puritan conservative America lashed back with the Prohibition Amendment (1919), and, in the light of the Russian Revolution, of anti-progressivist sentiment aimed at Blacks and at Jewish and Catholic immigrants. A quota system (1924) was established to curb immigration from all parts of the world except Western Europe.

THE NEW DEAL ERA AND WORLD WAR II

The Great Depression, set off by the stock market crash of 1929, within three years threw 14 million people out of work, reduced industrial production by two-thirds and the national income by one-half. Franklin D. Roosevelt, elected President in 1933, inaugurated his ambitious New Deal program of social safeguards against unchecked capitalism. Many new government agencies were created, such as the National Recovery, Agricultural Adjustment, and Works Progress Administrations, which sought to stimulate the economy while protecting the mass of ordinary consumers. Roosevelt's greatest piece of legislation, the Social Security Act, established basic social welfare standards. The United States achieved full status as a world power through its participation in World War II. It entered the war after the Japanese attack on Pearl Harbor in 1941. The decisive campaign was the D-Day offensive which began in 1944 with an invasion of France's Normandy coast. Ten months later Germany fell to the Allies. Japan submitted to unconditional surrender in August, 1945, after the atom-bomb explosions on Hiroshima and Nagasaki. At the Yalta Conference (1945) the U.S., Great Britain and the Soviet Union carved up the world into respective spheres of influence, but ideological differences between the Capitalist and the Communist blocs soon led to a mounting distrust whose outcome was the Cold War. Yet, despite the Cold War, the 1950s were a decade of social and economic upsurge, in which the baby boom led to a startling population increase of 30 million. During the Eisenhower administration (1953-1960) the Supreme Court declared racial segregation illegal, and gave rise to the Civil Rights Movement which systematically fought to dismantle the last vestiges of institutionalized racism.

FROM THE KENNEDY ERA TO TODAY

Dynamic young John F. Kennedy, elected President in 1960, in the three years before his assassination created the Peace Corps and the Alliance for Progress, in addition to championing NASA's moon-shot project and, in the wake of the disastrous Bay of Pigs incident (1961), sharply curtailing the Cold War with his policy of détente, which led to the nuclear test ban treaty of 1963. After John Kennedy's assassination, the nation plunged into the Vietnam War and a period of political, social and cultural upheaval. The baby boom generation, having come of age, rebelled against the traditional "American way of life", embracing instead such alternative life-styles as drugs, communal living, pacifism, free sexual expression, and sympathy with third-world cultures and with ethnic minorities at home. Martin Luther King and Robert Kennedy were both assassinated in 1968. Richard Nixon was elected in 1969 and reelected in 1972, but was forced to resign in 1974 because of the Watergate scandal.

Jimmy Carter, elected President in 1978, sponsored the Panama Canal treaty (1978) and coordinated the Egyptian-Israeli peace treaty (1979). Republican Ronald Reagan, elected for two consecutive terms (1980-88), pursued a program of radical tax and budget cuts. His greatest achievement was the nuclear arms reduction treaty he concluded with the by then crumbling Soviet Union. George Bush (1988-1992), his successor, for a brief time during the Persian Gulf War (1991), was seen as a hero, although toward the end of his term his popularity plunged because of the economic crisis induced by the excesses of the Reagan era. Democrat Bill Clinton, elected in 1992, confronted a world in which the Berlin Wall, along with the U.S.'s arch-enemy, the Soviet Union, had ceased to exist.

Pleasant Point, on *Cobscook Bay*, homeland to the
Passamaquoddy Indians.

Cape Elizabeth, site of scenic *Crescent Beach State Park* and
of *Portland Head Light*, Maine's most famous lighthouse.

Maine, a small state which nevertheless comprises one-half of all New England, lies at the extreme northeast of the U.S., just beneath the Canadian border. Early explorers called the area "The Main" to distinguish it from the offshore islands, so determining its official name.

The original inhabitants of Maine were the **Abnaki Indians**. The **Vikings** may have been the first Europeans to set foot on Maine around 1000 AD. The French under **Champlain** arrived in 1604 and set up a short-lived colony, followed by the English who finally drove the French out and established a permanent settlement after 1622. In the Revolutionary War period Maine joined Massachusetts in resisting the British. The region gained statehood in 1820, and thereafter its population and prosperity grew rapidly through the timber trade and shipbuilding. Today, Maine's slightly more than one million population includes groups chiefly of English, French-Canadian, Irish, Scottish, Italian and German backgrounds.

Maine is made up of four major geographic regions: a **coastal lowland**; an **interior hilly belt**; a portion of the Appalachians known as the **Longfellow Mountains**, whose highest point is **Mount Katahdin**;

and a **dissected upland**. Maine has about 5,000 rivers and streams, and over 2,500 lakes and ponds (the best-known of these being the **Sebago, Belgrades, Grands, Rangeleys**, and **Moosehead**). Its major rivers are the **Androscoggin, Kennebec, Penobscot, Saint Croix** and **Saint John**. Nearly 90% of Maine's land area is forest, made up principally of spruce-fir. Its abundant waterways and forests make Maine a haven for such wildlife as the black bear, beaver, fox, lynx and marten, as well as game animals and more than 300 varieties of birds.

Maine's best-known museums are the **Maine State Museum** in Augusta and the **Portland Museum of Art**. The state's oldest historic landmark is the **Old Gaol** in York (1653). Revolutionary War sites are found at **Fort Western** (1754), where Benedict Arnold led his troops against Quebec in 1775; and **Burnham Tavern Machias**, where colonists met in 1775 to plot the capture of the British ship *Margaretta*. Other landmarks are **Portland Head Light** (1791) and the **Wadsworth-Longfellow House** in Portland. Maine's rugged natural beauty - including its 26 state parks, and **Acadia National Park** - attract thousands of visitors annually.

A stable, a typical site in rural Vermont.

Vermont, the **"Green Mountain State"**, is the northwesternmost and second largest of the New England states, the most important agriculturally, and the only landlocked one. Vermont's longest river, **Otter Creek** in the **Champlain Valley**, extends about 100 miles, and its largest lake is **Lake Champlain**. Today about 70% of Vermont is forest land (primarily northern hardwoods), compared to only 30% a century ago, when farming predominated. Vermont's highest point, due east of **Burlington**, is **Mount Mansfield**, while its lowest is Lake Champlain. The Champlain Valley occupies much of northwestern Vermont. The **Taconic Mountains** extend along the New York border, and the famous **Green Mountains** lie to the east of the valleys, extending the entire length of the state. The eastern **Piedmont** region is Vermont's largest and also most diverse, while the rugged **Northeastern Highlands** region is the smallest. The state abounds in wildlife, including white-tailed deer, weasels, shrews, red foxes, Canadian lynx, bobcats, beavers, porcupines, snowshoe rabbits, fishers, coyotes and black bears, plus occasional moose and panthers, as well as spruce grouse, partridge and wild turkeys. Vermont

was originally hunting territory for various **Algonquin** and **Iroquois** tribes, and most Vermont Indian place names are of Algonquin origin. Following a temporary French settlement on **Isle la Motte** in Lake Champlain in 1666, the first permanent one was the British **Fort Dummer**, established in 1724. Massachusetts colony was initially granted the southern half of Vermont, though George II overruled its claim, defining Vermont's present boundaries in 1741. Jurisdictional disputes with New York colony over land grants were resolved by Vermont's participation in the Revolutionary War. Vermont territory was admitted to the Union as the 14th state on Mar. 4, 1791, after having existed as an independent republic for 14 years.

A series of factors, especially the opening (1823) of the **Champlain Canal** connecting Lake Champlain to the Hudson River, oriented Vermont commercially to the south and away from Canada. Vermont's major museums are: the **Shelburne Museum**, which has one of the major collections of Americana in the country plus a research library and the sidewheel steamer *Ticonderoga*; the **Fleming Museum** at the University of Vermont, which organizes art exhibits;

The **Green Mountains**, rich in spruce, maple, birch and beech, extend from north to south through central Vermont.

and the **Athenaeum** in St. Johnsbury, famous for its collection of 19th-century art. Smaller museums are: the **Brattleboro Museum and Art Center**; the **Southern Vermont Art Center** in Manchester; the **Wood Art Gallery** in Montpellier; the **American Precision Museum** at Windsor; the **Fairbanks Museum and Planetarium** in St. Johnsbury; and the **Vermont Museum**, run by the Vermont Historical Society, in Montpellier.

Vermont registers over 1,200 historic landmarks. The major ones are: the **Bennington Battle Monument**; the **Hubbardton Battlefield and Museum**; the birthplaces of Mormon founders **Joseph Smith** (Sharon) and **Brighham Young** (Whitingham); Windsor's **Old Constitution House**, where Vermont's first constitution was written in 1777; and the Revolutionary war fortifications on **Mount Independence** in Orwell, across the New York border from Fort Ticonderoga. Vermont has 34 state forests, 41 state parks, and over 40 ski resorts. Its major recreational areas include the **Green Mountain National Forest**, crossed by the **Appalachian Trail** and the **Long Trail**; and the **Lye Brook** and **Bristol Cliffs** wilderness areas.

*Sunset view of **Boston Bay**.*

***Boston Harbor**, one of the finest natural harbors in the United States, and New England's most important seaport.*

***USS Constitution**, ''Old Ironsides'', launched in 1794, a view of which can be had from the ramparts of **Copp's Hill Terrace**.*

BOSTON

Boston, the capital of Massachusetts and New England's largest city, lies on a hilly peninsula where the **Mystic** and **Charles** rivers flow into **Massachusetts Bay**. The city proper occupies 50 sq. miles, and its half-million population is ethnically and racially mixed: mainly Irish, Italians, French Canadians, Portuguese, Blacks and Chinese. Since the 17th century, when the first American public school, **Boston Latin School**, was founded, Boston has been one of America's foremost educational and cultural centers. The city has more than 50 institutions of higher learning, including **Northeastern University**, **Boston University**, the **New England Conservatory of Music**, **Harvard University** and the **Massachusetts Institute of Technology**. The **Boston Public Library**, opened in 1854, was the first free public library in the U.S. The **Boston Museum of Fine Arts** boasts one of the nation's major art collections. And the **Boston Symphony Orchestra** and the **Boston Pops** are among the nation's finest musical institutions. **Harvard University**, founded in 1636 in the Boston suburb of **Cambridge**, is the nation's oldest institution of higher learning, and a member of the Ivy League. The undergraduate **Harvard College** is for men, while **Radcliffe College**, founded in 1879, is for women. The Harvard campus includes the **William Hayes Fogg Art Museum, Busch-Reisinger Museum of Germanic Art and Culture, Museum of Comparative Zoology, Peabody Museum of Archeology and Ethnology**, the **Botanical Museum**, and the **Geological Museum**.

Boston settlement was founded by **Captain John Smith** in 1630. By 1700 the city was a principal center for shipbuilding, whaling, fishing, and commerce. Bostonians were in the vanguard of colonial struggle against England, which culminated in the **Boston Massacre** of 1770 and in the **Boston Tea Party** of 1773. After the Revolutionary War Boston undertook a profitable trade with China, and developed its

Beacon Hill, *the seat of Boston government for almost two centuries, the very heart of elegant old Boston.*

Old State House, *designed by Charles Bulfinch in the late 18th century in imitation of London's neo-classical Somerset House.*

manufacturing industries. During the 1840s the railroads linked Boston to the other parts of New England, while the influx of mainly Irish immigrants provided a new labor supply. Before the Civil War Boston was one of the chief centers of the antislavery movement. It was also the home of the Transcendentalist school of philosophy, headed by Ralph Waldo Emerson.

Boston is full of historical and cultural landmarks, of which we can mention here only a few. The **Washington Street Shopping District** has the *Old Corner Bookstore* (1718), the *Old South Meeting House* (1729), *King's Chapel* (1754), *St. Paul's Cathedral* (1820), *Old City Hall* (1865), *Kennedys "commercial palace"* (1872), and *Filene's department store* (1912). The **Government Center District** has the *Blackstone Block* with its 17th-century street layout, the *Union Oyster House* (1717), the *Ebenezer Hancock House* (1767), the *Faneuil Hall Marketplace* (1767), *Sears Crescent* (1816), and *City Hall* (1968).

North End has *Paul Revere House* (1677), *Pierce-Hichborn House* (1710), *Clough House* (1715), *Christ Church* (1723), and *St. Stephen's Church* (1804). The **Waterfront**, renovated into a commercial complex in the 1960s, has *Commercial Wharf* (1834), *Lewis Wharf* (1840), the *Custom House Block* (1847), *Mercantile Wharf* (1856), and the *McLauthlin Building* (1864). The **Custom House District**, once Boston's economic center, has Charles Bulfinch's *Broad Street buildings* (1805), the *Chadwick Lead Works* (1817), the *Architects Building* (1853), the *State Street Block* (1858), and the *Richards Building* (1867). The **Financial District**, the country's original banking center, includes the *Old State House* (1713), the *Church Green Building* (1873), the *Richardson Block* (1873), the *Bedford Buildings* (1876), the *Wigglesworth Building* (1873), the *International Trust Company Building* (1906), and the *Stock Exchange Building* (1984). The formerly industrial **Fort Point Channel**, now a center of galleries, museums and loft apartments, features *South Station* (1899), the Boston Tea Party ship *Big Beaver*, and the *Children's Museum* (1975). The **Theater District**, also home of Boston's Chinatown, contains such early theaters as the *Charles* (1839), the *Emerson Majestic* (1903), the *Shubert* (1910), the *Wilbur* (1914), the *Wang Center for the Performing Arts* (1925), and the *Paramount* (1932). **Bay Village**, birthplace of Edgar Allan Poe, features the *First Corps of Cadets Armory* (1897), and the *Youth's Companion Building* (1892). Historic **Beacon Hill**, with its variously styled 19th-century architecture, includes *State House* (1797), the *Second Harrison Gray Otis House* (1802), the *Nichols House Museum* (1804), the *Chester Harding House* (1808), the *Somerset Club* (1819), the *Francis Parkman House* (1830s), the *Boston Athenaeum* (1849), and the *Appleton-Parker Houses* (1888). **Back Bay**, America's best surviving example of French-style Victorian architecture, includes the *Gibson House Museum* (1860), the *Arlington Street Church* (1861), the *First Baptist Church* (1872), *Trinity Church* (1877), the *Boston Public Library* (1895), *Symphony Hall* (1900), *Horticultural Hall* (1901), the *Fuller Mansion* (1904), and the *Berkeley Building* (1905). The **South End**, once marshland filled in during the 19th century, includes the *Cyclorama Building* (1884) and the *Lawrence Model Lodging Houses* (1892). **Fenway**, developed in the 1890s, features the *New Riding Club* (1892), the *Massachusetts Historical Society* (1899), the *Isabella Stewart Gardner Museum* (1902), the *New England Conservatory of Music* (1904), and the *Museum of Fine Arts* (1909).

Charlestown is full of late 18th and early 19th-century architectural jewels, among which *Warren Tavern* (1780), *Steck House* (1790), *Timothy Thompson House* (1794), *John Larkin House* (1795), Thompson-Sawyer House (1805), *Round-Corner House* (1814), and *General Austin's Stone House* (1822).

Harvard Campus, *founded in 1636 in the Boston suburb of Cambridge, is the nation's oldest institution of higher learning.*

*Three splendid views of **Niagara Falls**; **American** and **Bridal Veil Falls**, **Horseshoe Falls**, respectively distinguish the US and Canadian borders along the Niagara Falls.*

NIAGARA FALLS

The **Niagara Falls**, separating upstate New York from the Canadian province of **Ontario**, are formed by the overflow of **Lake Erie** into **Lake Ontario** at the rate of 35,000 cubic liters per second. This prodigy of nature was first described in 1678 by **Father Louis Hennepin**, a missionary in the entourage of the French explorer **Robert La Salle**, as "the incredible cataract or cascade, which is without equal". Since then Niagara Falls have become one of the wonders of the world, attracting some 10 million visitors each year. While certain falls in Africa, South America and even New York State are taller, what makes Niagara so impressive is its amazing 950-meter wide span of water, which forms part of the world's longest unguarded stretch of border, with the **American** and **Bridal Veil Falls** on the American side, and the **Horseshoe Falls** on the Canadian. The first honeymooners to visit the Falls were **Jerome Bonaparte** (a relative of Napoleon I) and his bride, in 1803. Other illustrious 19th-century tourists were **Charles Dickens** and **Oscar Wilde**. The famous daredevil **Blondin** began his tightrope walks across the cascade in 1859, and subsequently repeated the stunt on stilts, turning cartwheels, pausing to cook dinner halfway, and carrying someone on his back. In 1901, **Annie Edson Taylor** became the first person to plunge over the Falls in a barrel and live. In the same carnival vein are the present-day museums devoted to **Houdini, Ripley's Believe It Or Not**, and **Louis Tussaud's wax figures**. In 1885 the Falls became the first national U.S. park, thanks to the efforts of **Frederick Law Olmstead**, planner of New York City's Central Park. The Falls can be explored in two ways. One is a boat-ride on the **Maid of the Mist**, a steamer that has been running almost uninterruptedly since 1846 and that navigates near the American and Bridal Veil Falls and nearly beneath the awful downpour of Horseshoe Falls with its furious blurring spray as the boat rolls against the current. The other is a long elevator ride and walk down beneath Bridal Veil to the **Cave of the Winds**, where the constant mist is often crossed by rainbows. The Falls are the biggest source of hydroelectric energy in the western hemisphere, feeding the gigantic **Robert Moses Niagara Power Plant** five miles downstream, from whose observatory, the **Power Vista**, twice as high as the Falls, one gets a gorgeous view of the panorama.

*Lower Manhattan: Battery Park at its tip, in back the **Financial District**, and skirting it the **South Ferry** piers for **Staten Island** and the cruise ship piers for sightseeing around the Bay.*

*The **Statue of Liberty**, most famous Symbol of America; the legendary **Empire State Building**; the typical 1930's spire of the **Chrysler Building**; the 110-storey **Twin Towers**.*

NEW YORK CITY

The fascination of **New York** lies in its schizoid extremes and contradictions, more intense by far than in any other American city. In **"the Big Apple"** you can find the ultimate heights and the depths of America: the poshness of **Fifth Avenue** just blocks from the poverty of **Harlem**; the Bohemian chicness of **Greenwich Village** and **SoHo** just a hop from the funky swarms of **Times Square** and the citadels of commerce of **Midtown** and the **Financial District**; on one end the wasteland of the **Bronx**, and on the other the striving middle-class sections of **Queens** and **Brooklyn**; the brash success of its yuppies and the fervid quest for the American dream of its newcomers from the provinces and abroad, amid the homeless and the **Bowery** derelicts. New York is the national and world capital of every branch of traditional, popular and avant-garde culture. It is a brutal and heartless city, yet a big-hearted city; crass and vulgar, yet super-refined and sophisticated; full of an insane frenetic energy, yet with oases of utter tranquillity; the epitomy of post-modern alienation, yet America's eternal melting pot, in which its multiracial multiethnic hordes jostle each other toward the goal of becoming Americans, while preserving the distinct flavors of their cultural origins. The hub of New York is of course **Manhattan** (from the Indian "Manahatta"), the city's original nucleus and the island borough that contains its most famous landmarks, from the **Statue of Liberty** and the **Empire State Building** to **Rockefeller Center**, the **Metropolitan Opera** and **Central Park**. The original 17th-century Dutch settlement of **New Amsterdam** was taken over by the British in 1664 and rebaptized as New York in 1686. After the Revolutionary War, New York served, from 1785 to 1790, as the first capital of the new American Republic, and until 1796 was the capital of New York State. Throughout the 18th and 19th centuries the city prospered, especially after the opening of the Erie Canal in 1825, and the influx of European immigrants from the 1840s on made

it grow to its present mammoth proportions. In 1896, Manhattan was linked to the Bronx, Brooklyn, Queens and Staten Island to form the five-borough municipality of **Greater New York**. The present population of New York is about 8 million, and four of its five boroughs could each vie as the most populous U.S. cities, if they were not part of the same bustling metropolis.

In Manhattan the lights never go out. The borough's night-life, as seen here in this view of **Midtown**, is illuminated by a speckled neon galaxy, like a Mondrian painting. Here the daytime frenzy never abates but takes on the gaudy dreamlike hues of raucous pleasures and entertainments in its theaters, nightclubs and restaurants, amid shadows where a million dramas are enacted and where the constant upkeep and industry demanded by this urban Leviathan are carried on, in preparation for the new day. At **Times Square**, once the home of Tin-Pan Alley and the Ziegfeld Follies, the flashing neon signs achieve the delirium of a pop-art happening. They are a jungle of blinding kitsch at the heart of the city's tawdry, legendary pleasure dome, its "red-light district", full of souvenir and eros shops and porno movie houses, where sex is sold, live and on celluloid, in a thousand

*The exciting neon lights of **Radio City**.*

*Night pop-art form: neon. **Times Square**, former hub of New York's theater district, is now the city's "Sodom-and-Gomorrah".*

*Rockefeller Center: a microcity skyscraper complex built in the 30's, home of the **RCA Building** and of **Radio City Music Hall**; the **Plaza** shown here in its winter function as an ice-skating rink.*

*Central Park, the 840-acre strip of landscaped greenery that stretches from **Columbus Circle** to **Harlem**.*

different formats, for every taste and pocketbook. The Square has been immortalized countless times, from Edward Steichen's famous photo of the 40s to Woody Allen's film *Old Radio Days*. The city's current Mayor, Rudolph Giuliani, has undertaken to "clean up" Times Square and replace its Sodom-and-Gomorrah with respectable offices, a mega record shop and a gorgeous music hall restructured by the Disney Corporation. Only time will tell if he is to succeed. **Rockefeller Center**, situated between 48th and 52nd Streets and between 5th and 6th Avenues, is a skyscraper and theater complex, with **Rockefeller Plaza** at its center. A masterpiece of art-deco architecture (it was concluded in 1939), the Center is considered "the finest spatial grouping of skyscrapers the world has seen". Its two most outstanding structures are the 70-storey **RCA Building** and **Radio City Music Hall.** In summer, the Plaza, with its famous gold Prometheus, hosts a chic outdoor café, and in winter an ice-skating rink and a giant Christmas tree, immortalized in many films, the latest *Home Alone 2: Lost in New York*. The complex also houses exhibit rooms, a broadcasting studio, and a network of underground streets and walkways with murals, statuary and sculptural decorations - a true microcity.

Lower Manhattan comprises much of the borough's industry and ethnic and artistic glamor. **The Battery** and the **Financial District**, with **City Hall**, the **Stock Exchange** and the **World Trade Center**, lie at its tip. **Brooklyn Bridge** and **Manhattan Bridge** span the mouth of the East River, linking up Lower Manhattan with the borough of **Brooklyn**. The Brooklyn Bridge, completed in 1883, was America's first great suspension bridge. Just in back of the Financial District is **Chinatown**, a still teeming mecca of oriental immigration, second only to its San Francisco counterpart. Next to it is **Little Italy**, a feisty "Neapolitan-style" neighborhood, famous for its **Feast of San Gennaro** and for its Italian restaurants, groceries and pastry shops. Just to the north is **Greenwich Village**, New York's traditional bohemian center, and home, at **Washington Square**, of **New York University**. To the east is **SoHo**, an area of chic artists' lofts, and the **East Village**, the bohemian frontier that rubs shoulders with a potpourri of ethnic populations, old and new, that stretch from **First Avenue** down to the East River, and include the still thriving Jewish neighborhood of the **Lower East Side**. Lower Manhattan ends at 14th Street, the southern border of **Midtown**.

The **Statue of Liberty**, best-known symbolic image of America, lies in **New York Harbor** just southwest of the **Battery**. Conceived by a French-American team of engineers and artists, among whom Gustave Eiffel who planned its inner wrought-iron pylon, the 150-foot high statue was a gift of the French government and was unveiled in 1886. The Statue of Liberty was the first stirring sight of America had by immigrants pouring in on the transatlantic steamers around the turn of the century. The promise of hope it offered is summed up in the inscripton at its base: "Give me your tired, your poor, your huddled masses, yearning to be free."

No trip to New York is complete without a spin around **Central Park** in a horse-drawn carriage. The 840-acre park was designed in the mid-19th century by landscape architects Frederick Olmsted and Calvert Vaux, and features walks, lakes, open fields, a **zoo**, the **Metropolitan Museum of Art**, the **Wollman Skating Rink** and the **Delacorte Theater**. **Columbus Circle** flanks the park's southern border, and **5th Avenue** and **Central Park West** run along its eastern and western perimeters. At its northern end is **Harlem**.

*Lower Manhattan, seen from Brooklyn, with the **Manhattan** and **Brooklyn Bridges**.*

The **Caesars Hotel Casino** and the **Trump Plaza Hotel Casino** at Atlantic City, two of the bustling gambling casinos, amidst the genteel family-run hotels of a former era.

ATLANTIC CITY

Atlantic City, located on the southeastern shores of New Jersey, at a site called **Absecon Beach**, has been an important northeastern resort town since the second half of the 1800s. A certain **Dr. Jonathan Pitney** was instrumental in getting the **Camden and Atlantic Railroad** to establish its eastern terminus there in 1852, and between 1870 and 1882 the town's first boardwalk and pier were built. The annual **Miss America Pageant** has been held there since 1921, amidst a sappy glitter of floats and - for many years - the throaty crooning of singer **Bert Parks**. Its modest hotels and beach cottages, and its overall sleepy atmosphere became passé after the Second World War, when air travel brought more distant exotic vacation places within easy reach. For three decades Atlantic City suffered a steady decline in tourism, frequented mainly by elderly "snowbirds" who couldn't afford to go south to Florida. Then, in the mid-70s, the state of New Jersey lifted its ban on gambling, and in the space of a few years Atlantic City was revitalized by the construction of a chain of **gaming casinos**, to become the **Las Vegas of the East Coast**. In the early 80s French film director Louis Malle shot his film *Atlantic City* on location there, an emblematic story of an aged small-time con man (played by a marvelous Burt Lancaster) who gets romantically involved with a pretty young woman (Susan Sarandon), against the backdrop of the town's tawdry haunts of beach, boardwalk, old boarding houses, amusement park, and gambling spots.

Liberty Bell, rung at the adoption of the Declaration of
Independence in 1776.

Clothespin, *City Hall*, completed around 1900, by some
considered a monstrosity and by others "the greatest
single effort of late 19th-century architecture".

The **Art Museum** has a major collection of medieval-to-
Renaissance art, as well as Oriental, American and
decorative artworks.

PHILADELPHIA

Philadelphia, the "city of brotherly love", is the
capital of **Pennsylvania** and its largest city, located in the southeastern part of the state on the
west bank of the **Delaware River**, with the **Schuylkill
River** flowing through its center. The city, with a population of about 1.5 million, ranks second in the country as a port of trade, and **Philadelphia International
Airport** is one of the nation's busiest. Philadelphia has
more than 30 institutions of higher learning, among
which the **University of Pennsylvania** (est. 1740 by
Benjamin Franklin) and **Temple University** (1884).
Philadelphia's major cultural institutions are the
Pennsylvania Academy of the Fine Arts, the
American Philosophical Society, and the **Academy
of Natural Sciences**. The **Philadelphia Orchestra**,
the **Pennsylvania Ballet**, and the **Opera Company of
Philadelphia** are world-famous. Museums include
the **Franklin Institute Science Museum** (with the **Fels
Planetarium**), the **Philadelphia Museum of Art**, the
University of Pennsylvania Museum, the **Rodin
Museum**, and the **Barnes Foundation Museum**. The

Philadelphia Zoo, founded in 1874, is the country's
oldest, and is noted in particular for the naturalistic
habitat designed for its bird collection and for the
largest feline exhibit in the U.S. Philadelphia was
founded in 1681 by the English Quaker **William Penn**
as the center of an ambitious colonizing plan for what
eventually became the state of Pennsylvania. Penn
signed peace treaties with the Delaware Indians, thus
enabling the Quakers and other religious dissenters
to settle the area, and the town quickly prospered.
Benjamin Franklin arrived in Philadelphia in 1723 as
a young man and went on to become the city's leading citizen. Philadelphia was the largest city of the
colonies at the start of the American Revolution, in
which it played a decisive role, serving as the seat of
the **Continental Congress** (which drew up the
Declaration of Independence and the **Constitution**),
the capital of the colonies during the **Revolutionary
War**, and the capital of the Republic from 1790 to
1800. Although outstripped in size by New York,
Philadelphia continued to grow during the 19th and

*A carriage ride is a wonderful way to visit the **Old City**.*

***Society Hill**, the historic heart of colonial Philadelphia.*

20th centuries through a massive influx of Italian and Irish immigration, added to later by large-scale Black migration from the South. Philadelphia's two greatest historic landmarks date from the colonial period. The first is **Independence Hall** (1748), the *Pennsylvania State House*, a fine example of colonial Georgian architecture recently restored to its original design. The second is the **Liberty Bell**, now housed in *Philadelphia's Liberty Bell pavilion*, which was first hung in 1753 in the Pennsylvania State House, and was rung at the adoption of the Declaration of Independence in 1776 and for every year afterwards until 1846, when a crack prevented it from being sounded anymore. Both are located in the **Old City**, America's "most historic square mile", which also includes Georgian-style *Carpenter's Hall* (1774), *Todd House* (1776), *Franklin Court* (1785), *Bishop White House* (1786), the *First Bank of the United States* (1797), the Greek-revival *Second Bank of the United States* (1824), *Library Hall* (1789; reconstructed in 1950), *Old City Hall* (1791), *Philosophical Hall* (1789), the *Philadelphia Exchange* (1834), *Franklin Square* (one of Penn's original five town plazas), the *Betsy Ross House*, and *Christ Church*. **Society Hill and**

Penn's Landing contains the largest concentration of colonial-period structures in the U.S., including *St. Joseph's Church* (1733), *St. Mary's Church* (1763), *Old St. Paul's Episcopal Church* (1761), *A Man Full of Trouble Tavern* (1759), the *Hill-Physick-Keith House* (1700s), *St. Peter's Episcopal Church* (1763), *Powel House* (1765), and *Old Pine Street Presbyterian Church* (1768). The **South-Street-and-Queen-Village** strip from Front Street to 6th is known as the "hippest street in town", full of boutiques, cafés and restaurants, while **Washington Square West** is a more sedate bohemian area of antiquaries, quaint restaurants and a few jazz spots, and **Rittenhouse** an even more sedate residential district. **City Hall-Downtown** boasts the massive *City Hall Building*, completed at the turn of the century, as well as many recently built skyscrapers. The **Museum District** is located along *Franklin Parkway*, a Bell-Epoque boulevard that stretches from City Hall to the Philadelphia Museum; behind the latter stretches 8,000-acre *Fairmount Park*, the nation's largest municipal park. Other interesting areas of Philadelphia are **University City**, and **South** and **North Philly**. And don't miss the surrounding **Pennsylvania Dutch Country** and **Valley Forge**!

Independence Hall, where the Founding Fathers assembled to draft the United States Constitution.

The **Philadelphia Exchange**, the nation's first stock exchange, designed by William Strickland and opened in 1834.

Swann Memorial Fountain, in Logan Square.

Capitol Hill, *a curious mix of elegant townhouses, imposing government buildings, renovated homes, modern edifices, and slums.*

WASHINGTON, D.C.

Washington, D.C., the capital of the United States, is located in and coincident with the **District of Columbia**, a federally owned area bounded on three sides by Maryland and on the fourth by Virginia. The city proper, whose population is roughly 640,000 (half a million Blacks, 172,000 whites, and small groups of Orientals and Hispanics), is the hub of the nation's eighth most populous metropolitan area, made up of some 3 million inhabitants. Washington has excellent air connections from **Washington National** and **Dulles International airports**, as well as rail service to New York and Boston, Chicago, and points south. The city is a nexus of the Interstate Highway System, with access by way of a beltway circling the city. The **"Metro"**, Washington's five-line subway system, is a cheap convenient way to get around town.

George Washington himself chose the site of the nation's permanent capital in 1791, at the geographic center of the 13 colonies, and the government was transferred there in 1800. **Pierre Charles L'Enfant's** original city plan envisioned the sites of the White House and the Capitol, and a grid street pattern crisscrossed by broad radial avenues, with plazas and rotundas earmarked for monuments. The barely completed city, captured and burned by the British during the War of 1812, was afterwards reconstructed, though its period of full development began only after the Civil War, continuing up through the 1930s and the post-war period. Washington is governed under the **Home Rule Act** of 1974, which provides for self-government under an elected mayor and city council. From 1874 to 1967 the city was goverened by a presidentially appointed board of commissioners. The District of Columbia is not properly a state, and its residents gained the right to vote in presidential elections only in 1961, obtaining limited representation in Congress ten years later.

With its impressive geometric layout, Washington is the only major planned city in the country. Its central **Mall** area is surrounded by the buildings which house the various branches of the **Federal Government**: the **Capitol** atop **Capitol Hill**, **the White House at 1600 Pennsylvania Avenue**, the **Supreme Court**, the **Library of Congress**, the **State Department**, the **Justice Department**, the **Federal Bureau of Investigation**, and several others.

Lincoln Memorial shows a seated care-worn Lincoln, flanked by his Gettysburg Address and his Second Inaugural Address.

The Mall, the heart of the nation's Capital, reflects Pierre L'Enfant's essential design for the new city of Washington.

Vietnam Memorial, two polished black-granite walls inscribed with the names of the more than 58,000 Americans who died in the Vietnam War.

Scattered among these buildings are the **Washington Monument** (1884); the **Lincoln** (1922) and the **Jefferson** (1943) **Memorials** on either side of the **Tidal Basin**, surrounded by rows of Japanese cherry trees; and the neo-Gothic facade of the **Smithsonian Institution**. The **Smithsonian Quadrangle**, located almost completely under the Mall, comprises the **National Museum of African Art** (once the home of Frederick Douglass), the **Arthur M. Sackler Gallery** and the **S. Dillon Ripley Center**, devoted to arts and industries, natural history, air and space, and history and technology. The **Pentagon** complex lies across the **Potomac River** in Virginia, next to **Arlington National Cemetery**.

Washington has four major museums: the **National Gallery of Art** (1937), which focuses on the major schools of European and American painting, sculpture, graphic arts, and decorative arts from the 12th through the 20th century; the **National Portrait Gallery** (1962), dedicated to portraits of people who have made important contributions to the United States; the **Hirshhorn Museum and Sculpture Garden** (1974), devoted exclusively to modern art; and the **Corcoran Gallery** (1869), containing paint-

ings by Americans ranging from the colonial period to the present. Other museums are the **Renwick Gallery**, the **Byzantine and pre-Columbian collections** at Dumbarton Oaks, the **Freer Gallery of Art**, and the **Phillips Collections**. The **Library of Congress** contains the world's largest collection of books, manuscripts, and documents; the **Folger Shakespeare Library** has one of the world's largest collections of Shakespeareana. The **National Archive** houses the nation's historic documents and treasures. Of historic interest are also Robert E. Lee's **Arlington House**, **Ford's Theatre** where President Lincoln was shot, the **Vietnam Veterans Memorial**, and the **Holocaust Memorial Museum**. Must-sees are the **American History** and the **Afro-American History** tours. The **Kennedy Center for the Performing Arts**, seat of the **National Symphony Orchestra**, hosts operatic, dramatic, dance, and film performances. The **Robert F. Kennedy Stadium** is the home of the Washington Redskins. Recreational facilities include the **National Arboretum**, the **National Zoological Park**, and a boat basin on the Potomac. Washington's major institutions of higher learning are **Georgetown**, **George Washington** and **Howard Universities**.

Freeways, symbol of Atlanta's status as transportation center of the Southeast.

State Capitol, a touch of old Southern gentility amidst Atlanta's futuristic skyline.

The **World of Coca Cola**: America's legendary soft drink was invented in 1886 by Dr. John Pemberton, who marketed it as an "Ideal Brain Tonic".

ATLANTA

Atlanta is the martyred city immortalized in *Gone with the Wind*, the city where **Coca-Cola** was invented, and the birthplace and burial site of civil rights leader **Martin Luther King**. But not only. With its over 2 million metropolitan population, it is the transportation, commercial and financial center of the souteastern U.S. (the regional headquarters of such top corporations as **Macy's and IBM**, and the **Federal Government** center of the southeast, plus having, in **Hartfield Airport**, the largest passenger terminal complex anywhere, and in **MARTA** one of the most modern subway systems in the country).

Atlanta is located in north central **Georgia**, in the rolling foothills of the **Blue Ridge Mountains**. The state of Georgia purchased the site from the **Creek Indians** in 1821, but the city came into being only with the arrival of the first railroad (1837); its original name was in fact **Terminus**. It was renamed **Marthasville** in 1843, and then **Atlanta** in 1847. In 1864 Atlanta was occupied by Union forces under **General Sherman**, who ordered it burned to the ground. After the Civil War, Atlanta regained its position as transportation center of the Southeast and became the **state capital** in 1868. In recent decades it has been the leading Southern city in instituting civil rights legislation. Atlanta's **skyline** is dominated by the modern beauty of skyscrapers of hotel, business and shopping complexes. Office structures dominate the picture, the most remarkable being the **Georgia Pacific Center** building with its tiers of red granite punctuated by rows of windows. The **State Capitol** (1884) contrasts the overall modernity with the old Southern gentility of its façade built of Indiana limestone, its interior of wood and Georgia marble, and its splendid dome dressed in 23-karat gold and topped by an allegorical statue representing Freedom. Other examples of traditional architecture are: the **Tullie Smith Plantation House** (1840), the Palladian-style **Swan House** (1928), and **"The Wren's Nest"** which once belonged to the author of *The Tales of Uncle Remus*. Atlanta is also the home of Ted Turner's **CNN Center**, a megastructure containing two office buildings, a modern hotel, shops, restaurants, and movie theaters under a single climate-controlled roof.

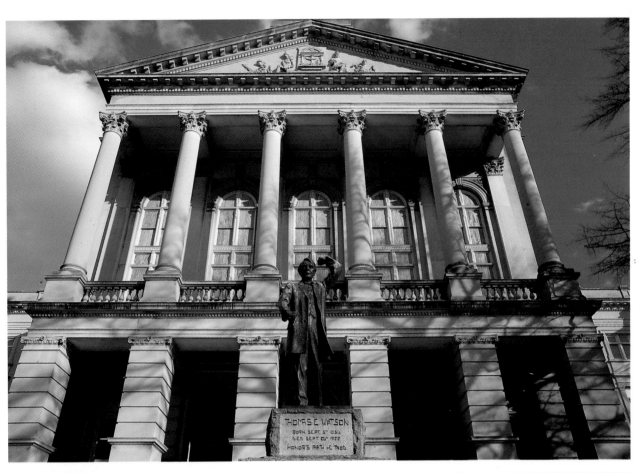

*Miami's skyline, Gateway to Latin America and the Caribbean, tropical tourist mecca, banking and manufacturing center, bordering the sea and the marvelous **Everglades**.*

***Bayside Marketplace**, Miami's recently built commercial and cultural complex, is right on **Biscayne Bay**. Featuring elegant boutiques and restaurants and open-air entertainment, it is a central meeting point for tourists and natives alike.*

***Ocean Drive** runs through the architecturally fascinating **Art Deco District**.*

MIAMI

Miami, called "the Magic City", is Florida's largest as well as culturally and commercially most important urban center, although the smaller **Tallahassee** in the north is actually the state capital. The city, together with the 27-municipality **Greater Miami Area** of which it is a part, has an overall population of three and a half million. This Greater Miami area lies at the mouth of the **Miami River** on **Biscayne Bay** in Southeastern Florida, covering more than 2,000 square miles. Miami's main industry is tourism, but its international banking and garment manufacturing activities are second only to New York's. In winter, Miami becomes the haven of the "snowbirds", the droves of tourists who migrate from the chilly north to bask in its tropical warmth. Miami's international airport and cruise ship seaport serve as North America's main departure points for all of Latin America and the Caribbean. The territory of Miami was once part of the **Everglades**, into which the **Seminole Indians**, its original inhabitants, have long

since retreated. Its name, in fact, possibly derives from two Seminole words: "maiha" (very big) and "mih" (it is so). Miami was incorporated officially as late as 1896, when the East Coast Railroad finally reached its shores, and the city enjoyed its first period of expansion only in the 1920s and '30s. Today Miami has a largely Hispanic and Caribbean flavor, due to the great influx of Cubans, Haitians and other Latin Americans over the past decades, and Spanish is the native language of almost half its inhabitants. Despite Miami's cosmopolitan composition, the city remains distinctively "southern" in its easygoing, provincial hospitality and in the small-town identity of the many local communities which comprise it. A few years ago the city government gave Miami an ecological overhaul, cleaning up its beaches and the Miami River, expanding its parks and embellishing its tourist facilities, while also passing more restrictive wildlife preservation laws to protect that marvel of tropical nature, the Everglades.

Miami Beach, with its white sandy shoreline stretching to the Atlantic Intercoastal Waterway to the west and the Atlantic Ocean to the east, is considered the "Sun and Fun Capital of the World". The city, incorporated in 1915, is constructed on 17 different islands and connected with Miami and the mainland by causeways across the bay. Already in the '20s Miami Beach gained fame as a holiday resort for its luxury hotels and golf courses. Nowadays its fine resort facilities make it a mecca for the "snowbirds", especially the many elderly retired persons, such a sizeable part of Florida's population, who make good use of the beautiful wooden walkway that runs along the clean uncrowded beaches. Elegant **Collins Avenue**, on the 10-mile long main island, is Miami Beach's most important street.

On **Virginia Key**, just north of **Key Biscayne**, is the **Miami Seaquarium**. Established in 1965, this sea-life complex is not just a public recreational or educational center, but also the site for important marine research, boasting the most successful breeding program for the endangered manatee or "sea cow". The Seaquarium's shows and exhibits are spread out over 60 acres, connected by a convenient monorail system. There is an aquarium which recreates the life of a tropical reef; a dolphin show which includes the star of the TV show "Flipper"; a sea lion show in the golden geodesic dome; a Killer Whale show; and shark tanks which get spine-tingling at feeding time. In the main building, there are over 30 tanks of tropical fish from the Caribbean and Atlantic in simulated natural settings. An Everglades exhibit takes visitors along a boardwalk through a mangrove forest with turtles, crocodiles, fish, tropical birds, and other swamp life. A "Birds of Paradise" exhibit permits visitors to handfeed cockatoos, macaws, parrots and other troprical birds. And two new exhibits allow a glimpse of life in a tropical rain forest and in tropical tidal pools. **Ocean Drive** runs through the fascinating **Art Deco District** at Miami Beach's southern end. This District includes more than 400 buildings constructed in the '30s in such eclectic architectural styles as Art Deco, Streamline Modern and Spanish Mediterranean Revival, with motifs derived from the ancient Egyptian, Mayan and Aztec cultures. The flamboyant buildings are painted in beautiful pastels, and the area is also a late-night hot spot with a hip after-hours scene.

*Sailboats and yachts along the exclusive **Coconut Grove waterfront** with downtown Miami in the far distance.*

***Miami beach**, with its clean, uncrowded, sandy shoreline, is a favorite spot of the "snowbirds".*

*The **Seven Mile Bridge** is the longest segmental bridge in the world (6.79 miles).*

*Key Largo's **John Pennekamp Coral Reef State Park** together with the **Key Largo National Marine Sanctuary**, are part of the only living coral reef within the continental U.S.*

*Ernest **Hemingway's House**, where the celebrated writer lived in the '30s and wrote his most famous works.*

THE FLORIDA KEYS

The **Florida Keys**, with their distinctively Bahaman flavor, are America's own spectacular piece of the Caribbean. The word "key" comes from the Spanish **"cayo"**, meaning a low-lying coral island or reef. In fact the Florida Keys are a string of such **coral islands**, stretching more than 180 miles from Miami's Bay of Biscayne into the Gulf of Mexico to a point only 90 miles from Cuba. **U.S. 1** connects the mainland with the first and largest of the Keys, Key Largo, 42 miles southwest of Miami. The highway then continues on for another 113 miles, connecting 32 islands with 42 bridges, until it finally dead-ends on the southernmost island of Key West. U.S. 1 was constructed in the late '30s on the remains of a 1912 railroad line which was destroyed by a hurricane in 1935. The **Seven Mile Bridge**, going south from **Marathon Key**, is the longest segmental bridge in the world (6.79 miles). The beautiful panoramic drive from **Key Largo** to **Key West**, with the deep-blue Atlantic on one side and the shallow turquoise of the Gulf on the other, takes about three hours. There are many nature sanctuaries and wildlife refuges throughout the Keys, the most fearsome denizens of which are the alligators and crocodiles. The Keys are ideal for **sailing, surfing, hiking and fishing**. Islamorada, the "purple isle", is considered **the "Sport-fishing Capital of the World"**, and hosts the **Theater of the Sea**, the second oldest marine park in the world. Key Largo is **the Sport-Diving Capital of the World**, and its **Pennekamp Coral Reef State Park**, together with the **Key Largo National Marine Sanctuary**, are part of the only living coral reef within the continental U.S. The largest city of the keys, and also the southernmost city in the continental U.S., is **Key West**. **Duval Street** is the heart of Key West, and offers a good example of the island's curious mix of 19th-century Bahaman and New England architecture. Two of Key West's main attractions are on **Whitehead Street**. At number 907 is the **Ernest Hemingway House**, where the celebrated writer lived in the '30s and wrote his most famous works. At number 205 is the **Audubon House and Gardens**, restored as a museum and filled with original 19th-century furnishings and prints by the great bird-naturalist and artist John Audubon, who lived there in 1832. Key West night life pulsates with Caribbean **island music**, from salsa and reggae to soca and calypso.

*The River, **"father of waters"**, second largest in the U.S. and third largest in the world.*

MISSISSIPPI RIVER

The legendary **Mississippi River**, the second largest U.S. river after the **Missouri** and the third largest in the world, in its 2,348 miles-long course flows, together with its tributaries, through 31 states, over 40% of the nation's territory. Long before the white man came the Mississippi was an important transportation artery for the North American Indians; its name, derived from the Algonquin language, means **"father of waters"**.

The Mississippi originates at an elevation of 1,463 ft. in **Lake Itasca**, Minnesota. After flowing through several glacial lakes to **Minneapolis-Saint Paul**, it is joined by the **Minnesota River**. Following this confluence, the Mississippi is lined on either side by 200-300-ft. bluffs. Between **Minneapolis** and **Saint Louis** the Mississippi branches off into the **Illinois**, **Chippewa**, **Black**, **Wisconsin**, **Saint Croix**, **Iowa**, **Des Moines** and **Rock River** tributaries which irrigate the nation's most fertile farmlands. At Saint Louis the Mississippi is joined from the west by the **Missouri River**, its longest tributary, and at **Cairo**, Illinois by the **Ohio River** from the east. South of

Cairo the Mississippi enters a wide 70-mile-long valley that was once part of the **Gulf of Mexico**. Afterwards the river proceeds 600 miles further downstream through its lower, geologically "old-age" stretch, where it is contained within natural sediment-formed levees. Beyond these levees the Mississippi, branching off to the west into the **Arkansas**, **Red**, and **White River** tributaries, meanders through low-lying flood plains to New Orleans and enters the Gulf of Mexico about 100 miles further south. Because of its annual 500 million-ton sediment deposits, the 100 sq.-mile Mississippi delta extends about 300 ft. each year. The lower section of the Mississippi is given periodically to disastrous flooding, the most famous being the catastrophic flood of 1927. Since then the Federal Government has built artificial levees and dredged waterways that drain floodwaters into the Gulf of Mexico.

The original **Indian tribes** living along the Mississippi were the **Ojibwa**, **Winnebago**, **Fox**, **Sauk**, **Choctaw**, **Chicasaw**, **Natchez** and **Alabama**. Spanish explorer **Hernando De Soto** was the first

Windsor Ruins, once a fine southern mansion which served as a landmark for river pilot Samuel Clemens.

*Vicksburg, home of a **National Military Park** - one of whose many memorials is shown (above, right) - and of the **Warren County Courthouse Museum** (below).*

European to see the Mississippi in 1541. In 1673 the Frenchmen **Marquette**, **Jolliet** and **La Salle** explored the river from the north, and La Salle, reaching the mouth of the Mississippi in 1682, claimed the whole valley for France. The western part of the basin was part of the Louisiana Purchase of 1803. It was explored by **Lewis and Clark**, though only in 1830 was the river's true source discovered by **Henry Schoolcraft**. Much of the central United States was settled along the river system, and with the advent of the steamboat in 1812 reliable river transport rapidly increased its traffic. The Union-won **Vicksburg Campaign** during the **Civil War** was fought for control of the river. Gradually the steamboats gave way to diesel, screw-driven towboats pushing barges.

Many sights of natural and man-made splendor grace the banks of the Mississippi. In **Minnesota** there are: **Lake Itasca National Park**; **Chippewa National Forest**; the cultural and industrial center of **Minneapolis**; **Fort Snelling**; **St. Paul**; and **Red Wing**. In **Missouri** there are: **Hannibal**, with its scenic bluffs, home of Tom Sawyer and Huck Finn and of

*The cotton plantations, the most enduring symbol of the **Old South**.*

__Longwood__ (left) and __Stanton Hall__ (below and right), two wealthy manses of the Old South, which __Natchez__ opens to the public in March and October, though some stay open all year round.

their creator Samuel Clemens; **Clarksville**, with its skylift ride to an ancient Indian burial ground and museum; **St. Louis**, with its soaring **Gateway Arch**; and the early 18th-century French settlement of Ste. Genevieve. In **Illinois** there is **Cairo** where the Ohio and Missouri Rivers join. In **Tennessee** there is **Memphis**, home of the blues. In **Mississippi** there are: the **Vicksburg National Military Park**, relic of the Civil War siege; the modern city of **Vicksburg** with its fine old homes, and the **Warren County Courthouse** which now serves as a Confederate museum; the **Florewood River Plantation** history park; the large stone columns of the **Windsor Ruins**, originally a fine southern mansion which served as a landmark for river pilot Samuel Clemens and was destroyed by fire in 1890; **Rowan Oak**, at **Oxford**, the home of William Faulkner; and **Natchez**, the oldest town on the river, with the old plantation home of **Longwood** and the excavated Indian site of **Grand Village**. In **Louisiana** there are: the state capital **Baton Rouge**; **Great River Road Plantations'** many ante-bellum "manses"; and of course **New Orleans**, home of jazz and Mardi Gras.

New Orleans Cathedral, in central Jackson Square, amid structures dating from the period of Spanish rule.

NEW ORLEANS

New Orleans, known as the **"Big Easy"**, is the city of **jazz** and **Mardi Gras**, the most cosmopolitan city of the South, and, together with San Francisco, the most "European" city of America, with its charming French and Spanish colonial architecture, and with the typically Latin tolerance of its racially mixed population. New Orleans lies at the southern edge of **Louisiana**, on the **Mississippi**, a hundred miles from the **Gulf of Mexico**. Most of it is situated on the river's east bank, with **Lake Pontchartrain** to the north. The present population is 558,000, and the inhabitants of the four-parish metropolitan area number more than a million. The climate is mild, with hot, humid summers. The **port of New Orleans** is one of the world's largest, and second in the United States. The **city's economy** is dominated by the petrochemical, aluminum and food-processing industries, but mainly by tourism. New Orleans was **founded in 1718** by Jean Baptiste Le Moyne, sieur de Bienville, and named for the regent of France, Philippe II, duc d'Orléans. The French, unable to make the colony profitable, abandoned it to the Spanish in 1763. In 1800, Spain ceded it back to France, then under the reign of Napoleon I. Thomas Jefferson, fearing Napoleon's imperialist designs, in 1803 negotiated to buy New Orleans, along with the entire Louisiana Territory, in what is known as the **Louisiana Purchase**. The **greatest cultural contribution** of New Orleans is **jazz**, in particular **Dixieland**, blended from the folk music of all its varied inhabitants; such jazz greats as Jelly Roll Morton, Sidney Bechet and Louis Armstrong were native New Orleanians. The city's **most important tourist event** is **Mardi Gras**, celebrated for a week before the start of Lent. Born more than a hundred years ago in the balls and parades of a private social club,

*Bourbon Street, in the **Vieux Carré**, famous for its jazz spots and strip joints.*

Mardi Gras has become a popular, city-wide event, and includes floats and jazz bands, culminating in the election of a "King and Queen", amid showers of baubles and doubloons tossed at the crowds which make their way through the French Quarter. New Orleans is also noted for its fine **restaurants**, and for its numerous **cultural facilities** and **institutions of higher learning** (among these, Tulane, Dillard and Loyola Universities). Even though **Bourbon Street**, the most famous street of the Vieux Carré, takes its name from the royal French house, today it alludes mainly to the cascades of liquor that constantly flow in its bars and bistros. The excitement of the New Orleans **jazz tradition** still lives on Bourbon Street, where every night you can hear jazz veterans play up a storm in the numerous jazz spots, such as **Preservation Hall**, the **Palm Court Jazz Café**, and the **Louis Armstrong Foundation Jazz Club**. Since

the '40s, Bourbon Street has also been famous for its **strip joints** (the most notable **Jelly Roll's** and the **Famous Door**), and hawkers offer enticing peeks from the street to lure you in. Perhaps the most memorable image of the Vieux Carré are its **cast-iron terraces** with their hanging plants, wedding-cake tiers of filigree, supported by sinuous colonettes, that run entirely around the building. The **La Branche Building**, constructed in 1840, and located at **700 Royal Street**, is probably the finest structure of this type, with its cast-iron galleries featuring a well-ordered pattern of oak leaves and acorns.

*The **La Branche Building**, finest example of the Vieux Carré's cast-iron terraced structures.*

*The **skyscrapers** along the port remind us that New Orleans is also a city of commerce.*

***Old-time steamboats**, leaving several times daily, take tourists on excursions along the Mississippi.*

*A riverboat weaves among the islets of the **Mississippi delta** south of New Orleans.*

*The **Memphis waterfront**, recalling the once bustling levees of this **"Cotton Capital of the World"***.

MEMPHIS

Memphis is firstly famous as the adopted city of **Elvis Presley** and as the city of jazz great **W.C. Handy**. Historic Memphis boasts some fine 19th-century homes, churches and other landmarks. There is the French-Victorian style **Fontaine House** (1870-71); the **Magevney Home** (1837); and the stucco-over-brick **Mallory-Neely House** (1852-59). Gothic style **St. Peter's Cathedral** (1854) is the oldest Catholic church in Memphis; the **First Methodist Church** (1887), built of Alabama limestone, Arkansas ironstone and gray granite; and **Calvary Episcopal Church** (1840), built of handmade clay bricks, the oldest surviving church in Memphis. **Schwab's** drygoods store (1876) on Beale St., is in part a museum of Memphis memorabilia. The **Orpheum Theater** (1890) hosted in its time Paderewski, Lillian Russel, Harry Houdini, John Philip Sousa, Sarah Bernhardt and Sally Rand. **S.H. Kress & Co.** (1896, 1927) was the first five-and-dime in the U.S. Finally, **Court Square Park** (1897) has as its centerpiece the **Hebe Fountain**, a copy of a Canova original. Memphis also has some interesting museums and parks. The **Memphis Brooks Museum of Art** (1955) hosts a collection of Italian painting. Then there is the Pink Palace and Museum's **Civil War Exhibit**. The **Memphis Zoological Gardens and Aquarium** (1905) features a new grand entrance (1991) with Egyptian hieroglphics and carvings, along with its monumental **Avenue of Animals**. **Audobon Park** (1947) includes the **Memphis Botanical Gardens**, the **Arboretum** and **Audubon Lake**. The **Dixon Gallery and Gardens** and the **Chucalissa Archeological Museum** feature exhibits on the area's early Indian life. **Mud Island's** multi-level **Mississippi River Museum** includes a full-sized walk-through 1870s packetboat and a union Gunboat, and its 5000-seat amphitheater presents everything from pageants to Broadway shows. The **Memphis waterfront**, paved with pre-Civil War cobblestones, recalls the once bustling levees of this **"Cotton Capital of the World"**, while the **Memphis Queen Line's** cruises reproduce the riverboat world of Mark Twain. The symbol of modern Memphis is the **Pyramid** (1991), a 22,000-seat sports and entertainment center rising 321 feet on the banks of the Mississippi River.

GREAT SMOKY MOUNTAINS NATIONAL PARK

Smoky Mountains National Park, at the climax of the **Appalachian Range**, was set up in 1926. Its lands, unlike the national parklands in the west, were privately owned and had first to be purchased. White settlement, begun in the 19th century, had depleted the wildlife and devastated the landscape, but conservationist policies since the 20s have once more repristinated the wilderness. The area was originally inhabited by the **Cherokee Indians**, who called it *Shaconage*, "the place of blue smoke" from the characteristic smoke-like haze which envelopes the mountains and suggested its name. They cultivated crops, hunted, and lived in mud-and-log cabins. After having been brutally removed to reservations in Oklahoma, they were subsequently allowed to return.

The high altitude of the Smokies simulates a climatic shift to the more northerly latitudes of Maine and Canada, so that the park provides a plant "laboratory" encompassing most of the major forest flora of the eastern U.S. This, and the fact that virgin forests are rare in the East, make it no wonder that the Great Smoky Mountains National Park has been designated an **International Biosphere Reserve**. Fertile soils and abundant rain have determined a rich variety of flora. In the coves broadleaf trees predominate, while along the crest there are conifer forests similar to those of central Canada.

Late April and early May are wild-flower and migratory-bird season, while June and July offer a spectacle of rhododendrons. Fall, however, is usually considered the best season, with its cool clear days ideal for hiking. Winter is peaceful, with fog often blanketing the conifers in frost. There are superb high-mountain views winding up through **Newfound Gap**, with a spur out to **Cingmans Dome** and its observation tower. But each of the park's 800 miles of trails offers a particular richness of landscape.

Aside from hiking, there are ten camping facilities, and many park streams provide fishing for rainbow and brown trout. From the Tennessee side the first stop is the **Sugarlands Visitor Center**; at **Cades Cove** there is another visitor center; and from the North Carolina side the first stop is the **Oconaluftee Visitor Center**.

*The **Smoky Mountains**, called by the Cherokees Shaconage, the place of blue smoke.*

*The **Meeting of the Waters Fountain** celebrates St. Louis' founding near the confluence of the Mississippi and Missouri rivers.*

*The **Arch**, St. Louis' most famous monument, commemorates its role as gateway to the West.*

ST. LOUIS

S t. Louis, famed for its blues and ragtime tradition, is, after New Orleans, the most "French" city of the U.S. Founded on the west bank of the Mississippi river just south of its confluence with the Missouri river by the French fur trader Pierre Laclède in 1764, the city was named for the patron saint of France. It was part of the **Louisiana Purchase** (1803) and became the focal point of river trade and later a prominent railway center, which together with its central geographical position made it the crossroads of western expansion. The current 1.2 million population of St. Louis prospers above all on the city's excellent transportation facilities which are second only to Chicago's.

This role of "gateway to the West" has been commemorated by St. Louis' most famous monument, the **Gateway Arch** (1965). Designed by Eero Saarinen,

the 630-foot high Arch is hollow, and visitors may ride up to a special enclosed viewing deck which affords spectacular views.

The city's second most famous monument is the **Meeting of the Waters Fountain** (1941), designed by Carl Milles. With its bronze mythic figures and lighted jets of water, the fountain portrays the confluence of the Missouri and Mississippi rivers.

The partially neoclassical **St. Louis Basilica** or **Old Cathedral** (1834) is the city's first cathedral and the oldest west of the Mississippi.

The nine-block **Laclède's Landing**, part of the original French settlement, has been converted into boutiques, galleries, offices, quaint restaurants and lively jazz clubs. The **Old Courthouse** (1839-1864), part of the **Jefferson National Expansion Memorial**, was the site of the 1847 Dred Scott slave trial.

The **Old Courthouse**, in the Greek Revival style.

Steamboats docked along the river next to the Gateway Arch.

Eads Bridge is the oldest St. Louis bridge to span the Mississippi.

A typical mural at **Laclède's Landing**, one of the last city areas to conserve the flavor of **Old St. Louis**.

St. Louis boasts one of the country's first skyscrapers, the 10-story terracotta-colored **Wainwright Building** (1891), designed by Louis Sullivan. It also has a number of architectural curiosities: the **City Hall**, modelled after its Parisian counterpart, the Hotel de Ville; the eclectically kitsch **Masonic Temple** and **Fox Theater** (1929); **Union Station** (1894), which looks like a Romanesque castle and now functions as a hotel; and the Byzantine-style **New Cathedral** (1914).
Forest Park, site of the 1904 World's Fair, hosts the **Art Museum**, the **Zoological Park**, the **Jefferson Memorial Building**, the **McDonnell Planetarium** and the **Science Center**.

*Central Chicago. Behind the boats moored at the **Marina** looms the skyline: at the left, the **Sears Tower**, and toward the right, the **John Hancock Building**, the diamond-shaped **Associates Center**, the **Prudential Building**, and the tall, white **Amoco Building**.*

*Chicago River in **Downtown**. At the far left is the **Hancock Building**; in the left foreground the **Chicago Sun-Times Building**; at center the **Wrigley Building**; and at the right the **Equitable Building**.*

CHICAGO

Chicago, the "Windy City", is the strategic midpoint of the North American continent, the trade and transportation center of the great prairie lands from the Mississippi to the Rockies and from Canada to Mexico. While also a city of **finance** and **culture**, Chicago is mainly a city of **industry**, a blue-collar town. It is the second largest city in the U.S., with **3 million inhabitants in the city proper** and more than **7 million in its six-county metropolitan area**, forty percent of which are Blacks, and the rest descendants of the European immigrants who came in the 19th century. Chicago is prominent for its position on the **waterway** that links the **Great Lakes** with the **Mississippi River**, America's enormous continental inland sea. Chicago's **chief products** are **iron and steel**. It is the headquarters of several of the world's largest publishing, advertising and public relations firms, as well as of the **Midwest Stock Exchange**; and it boasts the **busiest airport in the world, O'Hare Field**. Chicago started out as a land tract the United States bought from the Indians in 1795. The original settlement, a cluster of traders' shacks outside Fort Dearborn, became the focal point of westward expansion after the opening of the **Erie Canal in 1825**, and the **arrival in 1852 of the railroad** spurred the growth of the town's industries and population. The **Chicago Fire of 1871** devastated the burgeoning, largely timber-constructed city, which was rebuilt in stone. Chicago became the **seat of Cook County in 1881**, and was the **site of the World's Columbian Exposition in 1893**. A second major surge of growth took place toward the end of the century, when thousands of European immigrants settled in the city, which became a stage of

Chicago Tribune Tower.

*The **Presidential Towers**, a residential complex on West Madison.*

George Washington Monument, at Herald Square, was built in 1941 to commemorate the first U.S. President along with bankers Haym Salomon and Robert Morris, who helped finance the American Revolution.

*The 1454-ft **Sears Tower**, modern symbol of Chicago's merchandising might, is the tallest building in the world.*

labor struggles culminating in **the Haymarket Riot (1886) and the Pullman Strike (1894)**. Violence continued to mark Chicago during **Prohibition** (emblemized in the gangland career of Al Capone) and in the **anti-Vietnam-War riots of 1967**. The city's **cultural institutions** include: the **Chicago Art Insitute**, the **Museum of Contemporary Art**, the **Field Museum of Natural History**, the **Adler Planetarium**, the **Shedd Aquarium**, the **Museum of Science and Industry**, the **Chicago Civic Opera** and the **Chicago Symphony Orchestra**. It is the home of the **University of Chicago, the Illinois Institute of Technology, Northwestern University**

and the **Roman Catholic Loyolas and DePaul Universities**. Chicago is also important for its architectural wonders. The first steel-framework skyscraper, the Home Insurance Building, was built little more than a decade after the Great Fire, and from that pioneer experience, brought forward by William Le Baron Jenney and Louis Sullivan, the functionalist **Chicago School of Architecture** was born. Their work was followed by **Frank Lloyd Wright**, a designer mainly of private homes, and **Mies van der Rohe**, a designer mainly of skyscrapers.
The most famous architectural landmarks in Chicago are the **Wrigley Building** (1924) and the neo-Gothic **Tribune Tower** (1925), which stand on opposite sides of **Michigan Avenue**, at the beginning of the **Magnificent Mile**.
The contemporary skyline boasts many recent structures of worldwide reputation: the **Sears Tower**, the marble-clad **Amoco Building** and the **Hancock Center**, which are the three tallest buldings in the world; the **First National Bank Building**, and the pyramid-shaped **Britannica Building**; the twin towers of **Marina City**, the **Xerox Center**, van der Rohe's **IBM Regional Office**, the **Chicago Mercantile Exchange**, and the **Presidential Towers**.

Four presidents together, representing the nation's foundation, guiding principles, unity and manifest destiny.

*Profile view of **George Washington**, the nation's first President.*

Distant view from observation terrace.

MT. RUSHMORE

Mount Rushmore National Memorial, situated in the **Black Hills** of southwestern **South Dakota**, displays the 60-ft-high busts, carved in living granite, of the heads of four U.S. presidents: **George Washington**, **Thomas Jefferson**, **Abraham Lincoln** and **Theodore Roosevelt**. The colossal undertaking was begun, under Federal government sponsorship, in 1927, and completed in 1941, by **Gutzon Borglum**, and, after his death, by his son Lincoln. The project, requiring the removal 450,000 tons of rock with the help of bulldozers, explosives and pneumatic drills, depicts, in the countenances of the four presidents, the themes, respectively, of the nation's **foundation**, **guiding principles**, **unity** and **manifest destiny**. Perhaps to compensate for the monument's one-sided patriotism, another colossus was begun in 1948 by Borglum's pupil **Korczak Ziolkowski**: a 564-ft-high equestrian statue of **Crazy Horse**, the chief of the Sioux Indians who defeated Custer at the battle of the Little Big Horn. In this case as well, the work was carried on after the sculptor's death in 1982 by his children, and on its completion, around the year 2000, it will boast being the largest statue in the world.

*Sunset on **desert plateau**, one of the world's most striking geological spectacles.*

*View of **prairie** with scraggly trees, hallucinated emblems of the desert landscape.*

COLORADO PLATEAU

The **Colorado Plateau** is a 5,000-13,000-ft-high desert region that stretches from **Arizona** and **Utah** to **Colorado** and **New Mexico**, covering a more than 50,000-square-mile area. The southern **Rocky Mountains** and the **Rio Grande Valley** bound it on the east, and the **Great Basin** bounds it on the west.

The **Colorado River**, flowing north-south through it, has formed its main geological features: the **Grand Canyon**, **Bryce Canyon**, **Mesa Verde**, **Zion National Park**, the **Petrified Forest**, and the **Painted Desert**. 146-square-mile Petrified Forest National Park, founded in 1962 in eastern Arizona, has the world's largest group of fossilized trees, dating from the Triassic Period.

Within the Petrified Forest is Painted Desert, a badlands region, which takes its name from the layers of red and yellow sediment and multi-colored clays exposed by sand erosion.

*The bare landscape of the **Colorado Desert**.*

*The **Cliff Palace**, Mesa Verde's major "Classic Period" ruin.*

MESA VERDE NATIONAL PARK

Mesa Verde National Park, in southwestern Colorado, is a major site of the prehistoric cliff-dwelling Anasazi (meaning "ancient ones") Indians. The name *mesa verde*, Spanish for "green table", was suggested by the park's typical land formations of steep rock walls and flat table-like tops. The site's ruins and artifacts register a millennium of cultural development, divided into four periods. From the 1st to the 5th century AD, the **"Basket Makers"** inhabited caves and pit houses, growing beans, corn and squash on the mesa tops, and keeping domesticated dogs and turkeys. From the 5th to the mid-8th century the **"Modified Basket Makers"** introduced pottery and house construction. From the mid-8th to the 11th century, the **"Developmental Pueblo period"**, the Anasazi began building *pueblos*, rectangular, partitioned, communal houses of sandstone blocks rising two or three stories. The 12th to the beginning of the 14th century marks the **"Classic Pueblo period"**, when the Anasazi moved into the canyons and built, in eroded alcoves high on the rock walls, immense communal cliff dwellings of stone, mud mortar and wood. A large open terrace across the front of the pueblo was used for such daily activities as corngrinding and pottery-making. The original pit houses evolved into circular underground ceremonial chambers called **"kivas"**, best seen in Mesa Verde's major Classic Period ruin, the **Cliff Palace**. Other Classic Pueblo ruins are **Balcony House**, **Spruce Tree House**, and **Square Tower House**. In the 15th century the Mesa Verde inhabitants abandoned their settlements, whether because of hostilities with neighboring tribes, or prolonged drought or the depletion of fertile land. The dwellers probably joined similar peoples in today's Arizona and New Mexico, to become the modern **Pueblo Indians**.

These cliff dwellings, forgotten for centuries, were rediscovered at the end of the 19th century, first by pioneer photographer **William H. Jackson** in 1874, and then in 1888 by two cowboys after whom the park's two main areas, **Wetherill Mesa** and **Chalin Mesa**, are named. Mesa Verde also has an archeological museum which reconstructs the life of the Anasazi.

YELLOWSTONE NATIONAL PARK

Yellowstone National Park is the largest U.S. wilderness preserve, covering a 3,468-sq-mile area in eastern Idaho, southern Montana, and northwestern Wyoming. Most of the park rests on a 7-8 thousand-ft plateau in the **Rocky Mountains**. 11,358-ft **Eagle Peak** is its highest point.

Yellowstone is a remarkable geological phenomenon, a place where the earth's crust is so thin as to be a window on our planet's inner workings. 570 million years ago there began immense processes of erosion and uplifting which formed the Rocky Mountains and changed stream courses. Subsequent volcanic activity produced the volcanic rock that formed the **Absaroka** and **Washburn** ranges. The oldest rocks are the metamorphic, seen on the **Buffalo Plateau**, while sandstone and shale are found on **Mt. Everts**, the **Gallatin Mountains**, and around the **Snake River**. Yellowstone is most famous for its geothermal features, including some 200 geysers, 10,000 hot springs, and many fumaroles, the best known of which are the geyser **Old Faithful** and **Mammoth Hot Springs**.

The park has a great variety of wildlife, including elk, buffalo, moose, deer, bighorn sheep, antelope, coyote, and bear, as well as countless colorful birds, including bluebirds, robins, mountain chickadees, junco, killdeer, blue and red grouse, tanager, and finch.

Plantlife comprises aquatic, desert, and alpine types, plus four kinds of forests, and a great variety of wildflowers. Eighty percent of Yellowstone is forest land, mostly conifers, the lodgepole pine being the most prominent, and a few deciduous trees such as aspen. Most of the park is drained by the **Yellowstone River**. The great fire of 1988, which left about half of Yellowstone burned, was the worst natural disaster the park has endured. Yet the fires, with the nutrient-rich ash they produced, have favored a reinvigoration of the forests and animal life.

Campsite traces and stone artifacts indicate that humans inhabited Yellowstone as long ago as the last ice age. The area was used by several Indian groups, including the **Crow**, **Blackfeet**, **Shoshone**, and **Bannock**, and by the **Sheepeaters** who lived

Daisy Geyser, with its cobalt-blue clarity, is one of the park's major wonders.

The colorful **Morning Glory** geothermal spring is one of the most alluring photogenic sights of Yellowstone National Park.

Yellowstone Lake, America's largest mountain lake, home of gulls, white pelicans, double-crested cormorants, and Caspian terns.

The waters of the Yellowstone River plunge down Yellowstone's own Grand Canyon forming the spectacular **Lower Falls**.

there all year round. The **Minnetaree Sioux** were responsible for the park's name, calling the cliffs along the lower Yellowstone River *"Mi-tsi-a-da-zi"* or Rock Yellow Water, a name later echoed by French trappers who dubbed it *"Pierre Jaune"* or *"Roches Jaunes"*. The first white person to explore the area was **John Colter**, a member of the **Lewis and Clark Expedition**, in 1807. Trappers and prospectors ranged there throughout most of the 19th century. The first hot springs were claimed in 1871. In 1870 a government expedition began studying the area, and in 1872 Yellowstone was established as the first national park. The first tents and dirt-floor cabins were replaced by the hotel at Mammoth (1883) and the Fountain Hotel (1891), and the early stagecoach and wagon rides over rugged terrain were the norm until the **Grand Loop** was completed in 1905.

The 142-mile **Grand Loop Highway** connects the access roads from the park's five entrances and encompasses Yellowstone's best-known attractions. A standard Loop tour starts at **Mammoth Hot Springs**, proceeds to **Canyon**, and from there to **Fishing Bridge, Lake, Bridge Bay, West Thumb** and **Grant**, where it swings back around to **Old Faithful**. Between Mammoth and Canyon there is the **Petrified Tree**, **Lamar Valley** (a good place for viewing wildlife), **Tower Fall** and **Mount Washburn**. Canyon's chief lookouts are **Grand View, Inspiration Point**, and **Artist Point**. Lush **Hayden Valley** is a sanctuary for the park's wildlife. The **Mud Volcano** area offers unusual thermal features, and **Le Hardy Rapids** the July spectacle of jumping trout. **Yellowstone Lake** is the country's largest freshwater lake at such an elevation. **Isa Lake** straddles the **Continental Divide**, flowing into both the Atlantic and the Pacific. Other of the Old Faithful area's thermal features are **White Dome, Pink Cone, Narcissus, Steady Geysers**, and **Firehole Lake**. **Norris Geyser Basin** is a concentration of fumaroles, geysers, mudpots, and turbid pools.

Yellowstone's visitor centers exhibit different themes. The **Horace Albright Center** features Indian and pioneer artifacts. **Old Faithful's Center** explains how geysers work. The **Canyon Center** describes the area's natural history and geology. The **Grant Village Center** features a slide show about Yellowstone's heritage. **Norris Museum** explains hydrothermal plumbing and describes the algae and bacteria that live in hot water. **Madison Trailside Museum** describes the history of Yellowstone. The **Fishing Bridge Museum** features wildlife and geology exhibits.

*The beautiful scenery is perfectly reflected in the almost still waters of the **Snake River**.*

__Grand Teton__, carved by glaciers over aeons into spectacular fairytale shapes.

GRAND TETON NATIONAL PARK

Grand Teton National Park, in northeastern **Wyoming**, was founded between 1929 and 1950 as an extension of Yellowstone, and comprises the **Teton Mountain Range** and a 500-square-mile wilderness area in and around the tourist center of **Jackson Hole**. The **Teton Range** is a chain of the Rocky Mountains, extending south for 40 miles beneath Yellowstone. It began to take shape just 9 million years ago through a process of faulting, uplifting, and subsequent glacial erosion. Though small - only the **Grand Teton** exceeds an altitude of 13,000 ft - the Range is visually impressive because of its seemingly sheer rise out of the lakes at its base. The Tetons have been uplifted unevenly, pushed up steeply at its eastern edge and gradually sloping down to the **Teton Basin** in Idaho. Glaciers have carved the mountains into spectacular fairytale shapes. The gneisses and schists making up the Tetons are actually 30 times older than the mountains themselves. Humans have frequented the valley for 11,000 years, including the **Crow** and the **Sheepeater Shoshone**, who arrived in spring and stayed through late fall to hunt elk and deer, although the freezing winters made it impossi-

ble to live there year-round. **John Colter**, a member of the Lewis and Clark expedition, was the first white man to enter the Teton Valley, in 1807. Up to the 1840s fur trappers and traders ranged through the valley. Cattle raising was begun in 1884, but the first permanent settlers were the Mormons who built a community near **Snake River** in 1889. **James Stevenson** and his group, having separated from the **Hayden Expedition** then charting Yellowstone, first explored the Tetons in 1872. The park, with its 200 miles of trails, is ideal for hikers and cyclists, who can enjoy spectacular views of the **Snake** and **Gros Ventre** rivers, mountains, lakes and waterfalls. Many bird species live in the park, including bluebirds, woodpeckers, meadowlarks, grouse, hawks, ravens, ducks, geese, and even an occasional bald eagle and trumpeter swan. Other wildlife are bison, elk, moose, deer, and wolves. **Teton Village** boasts one of the nation's largest aerial ski trams, and **Jackson Hole ski resort** has more than 30 black diamond runs. Not to miss are Jackson Hole's wild west stagecoach ride, elk antler arch, boardwalks and Cowboy Bar, as well as its galleries and museums.

Salt Lake City, **capital of Utah and of the Mormon Nation,** *stands on a 4000-ft. high desert valley.*

Salt Lake Temple, *built of nine-foot thick granite blocks, and topped by the glittering gold statue of the Angel Moroni.*

SALT LAKE CITY

Salt Lake City, the capital of Utah, is located in the north-central part of the state on the **Jordan River**, and has a population of 160,000. The city was founded by the Mormon prophet **Brigham Young** in July 1847, as a religious sanctuary after years of persecution and hardship. He and his industrious followers planned a modern urban site with city blocks of 10 square acres and streets 132 feet wide. As a focal point Young built **Temple Square**, filled with historic buildings and gardens. The **Salt Lake Temple** itself took 40 years to build, starting in 1853. The best-known building in the square is the **Mormon Tabernacle**, an engineering marvel dating from 1867, constructed on principles derived from bridge engineering to create the self-supporting wooden-arched, lattice-beamed roof which covers an area 250 ft. by 150 ft. Also in Temple Square is **Assembly Hall**, a Gothic Revival building now used for concerts, as well as the **Seagull Monument**, dedicated to the flock of birds that saved the Mormon pioneers' first crops during a siege of voracious crickets. Near Temple Square stands the **Museum of Church History and Art**, which displays, among

other period artifacts, the first plow used in Salt Lake City. There is also **Beehive House** (1854), Brigham Young's residence, built of adobe bricks. On a hill north of downtown is the **Utah State Capitol**, and charming 19th-century houses grace the fruit-tree lined **Marmalade District**. The **Pioneer Memorial Museum** houses the city's largest collection of frontier memorabilia.

The **University of Utah** is famed as the place where the world's first heart transplant was performed. Perhaps the oldest department store in America is the city's **Zion Cooperative Mercantile Institution**, or ZCMI, which dates from 1868. Surrounding Salt Lake City is the **Wasatch Range**, a mountain backdrop providing spectacular settings for hiking, picnicking, fishing and winter skiing. **The Great Salt Lake**, at the city's northwestern edge, fed by four rivers and numerous streams which carry large amounts of dissolved minerals, has the highest salinity of any body of salt water except the Dead Sea. **Antelope Island State Park**, lying just offshore, is a haven of sand dunes, grasslands and rugged slopes, and a refuge for deer and buffalo.

The Windows, because of the perfect eye-shapes of its northern and southern exposures, is also called "The Spectacles".

The Delicate Arch, with its perfect slender Roman-arch shape, is the overriding symbol of Arches National Park.

ARCHES NATIONAL PARK

Arches National Park, on the southern border of **Utah**, offers one of the most spectacular geological mosaics in the whole world. While smaller than the **Grand Canyon**, it is equally awe-inspiring, and is unique unto itself. In distant geological eras tectonic uplifting brought a great variety of submarine strata to the surface; simultaneously, corrugation upset the previous order, while the various materials, according to their respective properties, were sculpted in different ways by the winds. Arches National Park contains more than **200 arches**, the highest concentration in the world, due to the combination of raw materials and types of erosion. The rock comprising the arches is mostly the 140 million-year-old, reddish-brown **Entrada Sandstone**. This stone is first encountered near the park entrance at **Courthouse Towers**, which is a complex of rocky monolithic walls either abutting each other or, as in the case of **The Organ**, isolated in the surrounding plain. These slender monoliths made possible the formation of all the arches.

Twenty miles further in, beyond the fascinating **Balanced Rock**, is the first significant concentration of arches, called **The Windows Section**. This in-

cludes **The Double Arch, The Ribbon Arch, The Cove Arch, The Turret Arch**, and other shapes such as **Elephant Butte, The Parade of Elephants** and **The Garden of Eden**, on a rise dominating the **Dry Mesa** to the east, with to the rear of it the often snowcapped **La Sal** mountain range. Another noteworthy formation, **The Turret Arch**, suggests an ancient fortified gate, while nearby **The Windows Arch**, North and South, because of its two eye-shaped openings, is called **"The Spectacles"**.

The Double Arch is the most spectacular element in the Windows Section; here the winds actually "excavated" the heart of a rocky nucleus, leaving just two big arches to crown the space. However, the overriding symbol of Arches National Park is **The Delicate Arch**, with its perfect shape and its position atop a small natural amphitheater. The Delicate Arch can be reached along a splendid mile-and-a-half hike from **Wolfe Ranch**, or by car to a vista above it on its far side.

By contrast, **Landscape Arch** is famous for the recklessness of its balance, with its tapering vault, like a long bridge, through which a vast stretch of countryside toward the east can be seen.

Buck Canyon, sculpted by the mighty *Colorado River*, is 700 meters deep.

CANYONLANDS NATIONAL PARK

Among all the National Parks of America's Southwest, **Canyonlands** provides the most variegated combination of geological fantasies. As opposed to **Arches Park**, Canyonlands' morphological typologies cover the entire region. The structural backbone of Canyonlands is the confluence of the smaller **Green River** into the mighty **Colorado River**. Though usually peaceful, these rivers can suddenly become violent after heavy rainfall or seasonal changes in the upstream regions, and they vent their destructive fury on fragile, sedimentary soils. Thus the waters have cut deep down into the soil, widening lateral valleys and multiplying the river bends and fluvial terraces to produce three distinct regions: between the two waterways, **Island in the Sky**; to the east, **The Needles**, an uneven, deeply eroded area with infinite morphological fantasies among peaks and natural arches; and to the west, **The Maze**, a vast alluvial plain cut into by a wide variety of canyons. The signs of the Colorado's erosive work can be seen, on the eastern side of the Island in the Sky, along the vast furrowed **White Rim** plain, in the silhouette of **Buck Canyon**, 700 meters deep. The two rivers take on different colors from the types

and abundance of detritus swept along them. Before leaving the Park's boundaries the Colorado passes through the **Mile Long Rapids**, and right afterwards the **Big Drop Rapids**, two of the most violent stretches of its course, and formidable challenges for the most expert rafter.

The left side of the Island in the Sky dominates the last stretch of the Green River, which despite its smaller size has caused greater erosion into the body of the White Rim. The waters enter in the north, at **Labyrinth Canyon**, in the shadow of **The Spur**, the vast tableland in the **Glen Canyon Recreation Area**, and enter their last stretch through **Stillwater Canyon**. From the heights of **Green River Overlook** and **Murphy Point**, this conformation appears in all its grandiose simplicity, especially in the cruel split near **Soda Springs Basin**. Notwithstanding these two great rivers, drought is a constant reality in the Canyonlands. The highest part of Island in the Sky - crater-shaped **Upheaval Dome**, **Grand View** and **Mesa Arch** - commands spectacular views of the whole region. While Island in the Sky is accessible by car, The Needles can only be explored on foot, and The Maze requires a land rover.

MONUMENT VALLEY

The image of these natural monuments sculpted in rock, fragile monoliths lost in an infinite horizon, has become the universal symbol of the American West, exploited by Wild West films from the 30s on as the ideal stage of heroically spacious desolation on which to recite the saga of the American frontier. Situated a little south of the final stretch of the San Juan River, near its Goosenecks, the **Monument Valley** contains typically red-colored cliffs of the **Cutler Formation**, 280 million-year-old rock layers formed from the residue of mountains just partially solidified and thus prey to early erosion. The successive tectonic risng and motion have produced fractures accelerating the work of rain and wind.

The more solid layers of sandstone act as pedestals or **"buttes"** for the more fragile formations, until they too are worn away and the overlying rocks crumble into fragments at the foot of the **Mesas**. Though the region is usually arid, the rains, when they arrive, are torrential and turn the small valley into a flooded basin. Monument Valley is actually a mountainous environment, nearly 5700 feet above sea level, and on the plateau the clouds from the Pacific are always in motion, though in summer the wind from the south heats the air to highs of 110°F. The presence of settlers in the valley has always been limited. The **Anasazi Indians** lived there until about 1300, followed by the **Navajo** sheepherders, and for a brief time white prospectors during the shortlived **Gold Rush**. Monument Valley remains today part of the **Navajo Indian Reservation**. From the **Visitor Center**, or **Mitten View Outlook**, one looks down on two semi-oval rocks rising up in the foreground, and on a more distant, astoundingly vast rock formation. **Mitten Butte** is made up of **West Mitten Butte** to the left (1000 ft. high), **East Mitten Butte** in the center, and **Merrick Butte** to the right, all three flanked by **Sentinel Mesa** and **Mitchell Mesa**. **West Gypsum Creek**, branching out along the plateau's eastward incline, is the principal source of the Valley's erosion. From the pedestal of **Elephant Butte** one faces huge Mitchell Mesa whose summit is so large that a landing strip has been constructed on it. Across the fields from there are the **Rain God** and **Tunderbird Mesas**. The Valley closes at **Totem Pole**, an imposing rock tower isolated in a field of sand.

West Mitten Butte, East Mitten Butte and Merrik Butte, so vast the eye can barely encompass them.

Gregory Butte, a mountain rising out of the waters of **Last Chance Bay**.

LAKE POWELL

Lake Powell came into being in 1956 with the construction of the **Glen Canyon Dam**, which by man's work turned the canyon overnight into a surrealistic seascape where up to then the only architect had been nature. The Glen Canyon project was part of an overall plan to exploit the water resources of the **Colorado River**, needed to foster the economic development of Utah, Colorado, New Mexico and Wyoming. Work began on the dam in 1956, at over 710 feet below the canyon's surface. Diversion of the river's course began in 1959, and the waters began pouring into the artificial basin in 1963, though it was completely filled only in 1980. The Glen Canyon Dam is second only to the **Hoover Dam** in size and capacity, rising to 638 feet over the river's original height. To facilitate work on the dam, the **Glen Canyon Bridge** had to be built across the opposing walls of the canyon; its 1271-foot span makes it the world's second highest steel arch bridge. Lake Powell was named for **John Wesley Powell**, a Civil War major who explored the entire course of the Colorado River by boat in 1869, accurately de-

scribing the places he saw and pointing out the region's environmental wealth. Powell proposed that Congress annex these territories, and as a result the **U.S. Bureau of Reclamation** was created.
Although **Lake Mead** is actually larger than Lake Powell, the latter's 186-mile length makes it seem interminable. At its maximum level the basin occupies a surface area of 252 square miles. The dam's **Power Plant** can generate 1,352,000 kilowatts, energy which is used throughout the neighboring states. In order to safeguard the region's environmental integrity, the **Glen Canyon National Recreation Area** was created, and covers the entire lake surface plus the entire route of the Colorado River to the boundaries of the **Canyonlands** and **Capitol Reef National Park**. The **Carl Hayden Visitor Center** atop the dam (named after the U.S. senator who fought throughout his long career to realize the project) provides spectacular views of the complex and a multimedia informational exhibit.
The original inhabitants of Glen Canyon were the **Anasazi Indians**, farmers and cliff dwellers who lived there from about the start of the Christian era

and abandoned it around 1300 A.D., to be replaced by the sheepherding **Navajos**. Franciscan missionaries explored the region in the 18th century, discovering a fording point called **Crossing of the Fathers**. But the great influx of white settlers came only with the **Mormons** during the mid-19th century, reaching its peak in the ten-year **Gold Rush** of the 1880s, after which the canyon returned to its former peaceful state, until the 20th century when it became a tourist attraction and the dam was built.

The **Escalante River**, a major tributary of the **Colorado**, runs through an area of still untouched canyon country, giving an idea of what Glen Canyon was like before the dam was built. While this area affords the possibility of long hikes into the backcountry, the most common means of exploring **Glen Canyon** is by boat - including a well-equipped houseboat which can be rented - from the principal docking base of **Wahweap Marina**, with the convenience of four other supply posts down canyon. The first place to visit is **Lone Rock**, a monolith the waters have turned into an island butte. One can then follow the original Colorado River channel to **Padre Bay**, with its outcroppings of **Gunsight Butte** and **Dominguez Butte**, also the site of the **Crossing of the Fathers**, which is now underwater. Beyond this is **Last Chance Bay** with its massive **Gregory Butte**, a mountain in the center of the waters.

Then follow **Cornerstone Canyon** and **Dangling Rope Marina**. Shortly afterwards the narrow **Forbidding Canyon** leads to **Rainbow Bridge**, the world's largest natural bridge, rising 290 feet and spanning 275 feet, once a sacred place for the Navajo, the Ute, the Hopi and the Paiute Indians, and so startlingly regular and imposing that one can hardly believe it is not mad-made.

Southward is **Navajo Mountain** (10,388 feet high) which often attracts clouds in an otherwise sunny sky. **Wilson Mesa** divides the **Colorado** from the **San Juan River** which one may detour on to reach **Hole in the Rock**, the legendary pioneer crossing opposite **Cottonwood Canyon**. **Lake Powell** ends, and the **Colorado River** takes up again, after **Hite Bridge** in the original Gold Rush area.

__Rainbow Bridge__, the world's largest natural bridge, so perfectly shaped and imposing that it hardly seems a work of nature.

CAPITOL REEF NATIONAL PARK

Capitol Reef, celebrated for its wall of stone that rises up like a barrier in the vast high plateau to the west of **Canyonlands** and to the south of **Arches National Park**, is the product of a great and unique tectonic uplifting. The stippled colors of the exposed strata are so bright as to recall a canvas by Cézanne.

The name **"reef"** stems from its barrier-like shape, while **"capitol"** stems from one of the formations, the **Capitol Dome**, whose shape and color are reminiscent of Washington's Capitol Hill.

The Park's formations range from the ancient **Cutler Formation** (270 million years old) to the **Mancos Shale** (70 million years old), and present a rare instance of crystal-clear geological cross-sections illustrating their history. The Park's territory is narrow, owing to the long combination of stratigraphs which have developed from north to south for 160 kilometers. The **Burr Trail Road** leaves from **Boulder** and climbs over 60 rough kilometers to the trail which from Notom flanks and then enters Capitol Reef's southern continuation, **Waterpocket Fold**.

Further south is **Cathedral Valley**, a desert area rich in bold sedimentary formations.

The **Fremont River**, which channels through the Reef, facilitated human access.

After the vast area of wooded plateaux at the entrance to **Bryce Canyon National Park**, the countryside becomes more barren, and high grounds with red-ochre tints gradually rear up.

The route is so dominated by the great walls of rock that to get to the **Visitor Center** one must flank the Fremont River.

The heart of Capitol Reef is formed by the daring stratified shapes of **Navajo Sandstone**, the **Kayenta Formation**, and **Wingate Sandstone**. Some of the more spectacular formations are the **Egyptian Temple**, **Capitol Gorge**, the **Golden Throne** and the **Chimney Rock**.

On many canyon walls the **Fremont Indians**, who inhabited the area from 800 to 1200 A.D., have left splendid **petroglyphs** depicting hunting scenes.

After 1880 **Mormon** groups settled in the area between the **Fremont River** and **Sulphur Creek**, and later cattle-herders occupied the **Capitol Gorge**, but the harsh environment eventually drove them away, and only the tiny village of **Fruita** still stands today.

Capitol Dome, so named because its shape and color are reminiscent of Washington's Capitol Hill.

Bryce Canyon, whose rugged and hostile scenery well merits the name of *"Badlands"*.

BRYCE CANYON NATIONAL PARK

The road leading to **Bryce Canyon** climbs to the top of **Paunsaugunt Plateau**, flanked by the pines and aspens of **Dixie National Forest**. It then follows the rim of the canyon, with various observation points overlooking the valley below. The first place to see is the spectacular **Bryce Amphitheater**. Afar off behind **Sunrise Point** and **Sunset Point** (named for the beauty of the light at those times of day), stretches the agricultural plain of Tropic, and in between bristle a world of rugged pinnacle-like shapes.

The **Wasatch Formation**, whose "bedding planes", with their varying geological ages and rates of erosion, have determined these jagged forms suggestive of weathered gravestones in a massive cemetery, gave the area its merited name of **Badlands**. Right below Sunset Point is Thor's Hammer, so named because of its size and shape. To the south side of the amphitheater there are also **Inspiration Point** and **Bryce Point**, where the landscape is more rugged still. Three trails - the circular Fairyland, the Queen's Garden and the Navajo - go from Sunrise and Sunset Points towards the **Valley of Tropic**, though under **Inspiration Point** it becomes an impenetrable jungle. The dense group of spires next to Sunset Point is called **Silent City**. The top of a spur below it is known as **The Cathedral**, while the towers at the back, connected with fissures in between, has the apt name of the **Wall of Windows**. From Sunset Point, the **Navajo Trail** approaches the slender figure of **The Sentinel**, and proceeds along the so-called **Whiteman Bench**, through the forest, from which one gets occasional glimpses of the **Pink Cliffs**. The same sculpted rock formation looks drastically different in winter and in summer light. An important element is the snow brought by the storms which streak across the **Rockies** and may last for months. **Winter dawn** is the most magic time of all: the soft mantle clothing the slopes now muffles the dense shadows of the fir trees which in summer lie dark on the canyon floor. After **Fairview Point** there is **Natural Bridge**, which because of its size and shape is one of the park's most stunning formations. **Agua Canyon** is the next observation point, with its panorama over the **Paria Valley** and the green of the Dixie National Forest. At its end, the rim on the Pink Cliffs separates into two lookouts called **Rainbow Point** and **Yovimpa Point**.

ZION NATIONAL PARK

The entire **Zion Canyon** environment can be seen from the east, a sweeping panorama of the **White Cliffs**, the solidified sand dunes called **Hoodoos**, the sparse vegetation, and the smooth-topped mesas. The **Pine Creek** road leads into the canyon through the **Tunnel**, winding down the southern side of the valley.

Near the **Sentinel**, **Mount Spry** dominates the canyon entrance. The **Great Arch** rises up in the highest corner of the vermilion wall of stone. Most visitors, though, come from the south, between the **Watchman** to the east and **Mount Kinesava** to the west, stopping at the **Zion Canyon Visitor Center**, just outside of which are two principal landmarks, the 6545 ft. **Watchman** monolith and the **Towers of the Virgin**. The highest peak, 7505 ft., is the **Altar of Sacrifice**. But the heart of Zion Canyon starts between Mount Spry and The Sentinel, with the impressive formations of the **Three Patriarchs**: **Abraham**, **Isaac** and **Jacob**. On the other side of the valley the cliffs rise up sheer; the most striking peak is the **Mountain of the Sun** (6722 ft.), distinguished by its **Hanging Valleys**, riverbeds hollowed out in the form of lateral valleys by seasonal torrents. **Zion Lodge** is at the canyon's center, where the valley is rich in vegetation and makes a perfect base for hiking or horseback excursions, one of which is to the **Emerald Pools**.

The **Virgin River** winds around **The Organ**, a diaphragm of brown that has resisted the river's erosive force, diverting its course. But the main feature are the two colossi of **Angels Landing** and **The Great White Throne**, which dominate the narrowing of the Canyon on either side. The latter is a

*The **Three Patriarchs**, Abraham, Isaac and Jacob, loom up imposingly over the Court of the Patriarchs.*

*The **White Cliffs** probably owe the typical white color of their crests to the sedimentation of marine deposits in some remote geological period.*

*The imposing mass of **Angel's Landing** - imaginary landing ramp for some divinity - dominates the left bank of the **Virgin River**.*

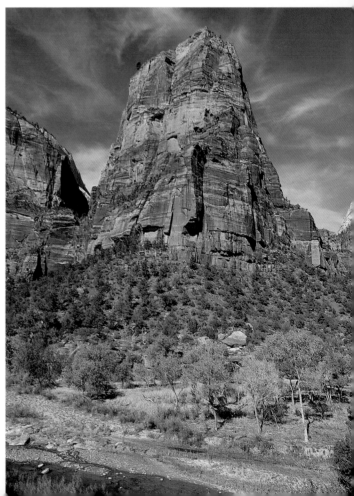

base for excursions to hidden corners of the valley, and the starting point of a trail back up to the Canyon's rim.

The inexhaustible water reserve in Zion Canyon is due to the extreme porosity of **Navajo sandstone**, an example being **Weeping Rock** which forms an extensive dripping waterfall that nourishes its "hanging gardens". Before the Virgin River disappears, it runs through a gigantic amphitheater whose monoliths practically form a ceiling overhead, an impressive site named the **Temple of Sinawava**. When the water level is low one can climb up inside these incredible surroundings, walking in the pebbly riverbed itself.

The Narrows mark the end of Zion Canyon, but the **National Park** continues for miles around in order to protect the Hoodoos and other minor canyons.

Mohave Point (South Rim) is an excellent viewpoint to admire three sets of rapids: Hermit Creek, Granite Creek and Salt Creek.

*South Rim: **Desert View**, first arrival point for many visitors; **Mather Point**, where most visitors get their first view of this "Seventh Wonder of the Natural World".*

*North Rim: **Point Imperial**, the Canyon's easternmost viewpoint, overlooks the **East Kaibab Monocline** at 2,470 ft above the Colorado River; **Cape Royal** promontory, with its view of the ponderosas giving way to more desert-like vegetation.*

GRAND CANYON NATIONAL PARK

The **Grand Canyon**, one of the geological wonders of the world, has been sinking and rising for millions of years. It last began to rise some 200 million years ago, and the **Colorado River** has been carving through it to reveal older and older layers of rocks. Its first human inhabitants were **prehistoric Indians** who lived there some 4,000 years ago. The **Anasazi** or **Pueblos** arrived some 2,500 years later, but about 1150 A.D. all settlements were abandoned, perhaps because of drought. Near 1300 A.D. the **Cerbat** people moved to the high plateaus, while the **Paiute** colonized the northern rim. In 1540 **Coronado** sent a brief expedition into the Canyon, and in the 18th century **Father Francisco Garces** spent several days there, but the white man fully explored it only in the mid-19th century, most notably **Major John Wesley Powell**. In 1919 the Canyon became a **National Monument**. The **South Rim** at **Desert View** is the first arrival point for many visi-

tors. To the west is the **Marble Platform** and the **Painted Desert**, and to the east the **Little Colorado**. **Lipan Point** is the trailhead of **Tanner Trail** to the mouth of **Unkar Creek**, on whose delta are thousand-year-old **Anasazi** ruins. The museum at **Tusayan Ruins** has exhibits on the area's Native American cultures. The view of the Canyon from **Grandview Point** extends from **Desert View** in the east to **Shoshone Point** in the west. On the far bank of the river is **Vishnu Schist**, the area's two-billion-year-old bedrock. **Yaki Point** is at the center section of the Grand Canyon. Across from it is **Wotan's Throne**, just to the right **Vishnu Temple**, and down below the gentle slope of the **Tonto Platform**. The **South Rim Forest** is dominated by the pinyon pine, the Utah juniper and associated high desert plants. Visitors likely get their first breathtaking view of Grand Canyon from **Mather Point**. From **Yavapai Point** well over half of the Grand Canyon can be

North Rim lodging complex, at Bright Angel Point, has Park Ranger stations, information centers, auto service facilites, campgrounds and store.

Havasu Falls, on the South Rim, are formed by Havasu Creek, a great tourist attraction; along it a rugged mile-long path runs up to the Colorado River.

seen. The **Yavapai Museum**, devoted to the Canyon's geology, provides panoramic observation windows. The **Grand Canyon Village**, originally a mining town, has become the chief visitor center, where many historic structures still survive. The **Powell Memorial** commemorates Major John Wesley Powell's explorations of the Grand Canyon. **Maricopa Point** is the western end of the **Rim Trail** from **Mather Point** to **Hermit's Rest**, and between it and the **Indian Gardens** plateau is a large red-rock formation named **The Battleship**. Also visible from this overlook is the dark **Vishnu Schist**. **Mohave Point** offers views of the **Hermit**, **Granite** and **Salt Creek** rapids. Farther along the **Rim Drive** is **The Abyss**, where the **Great Mohave Wall** drops 900 meters to the head of **Monument Creek** on the **Tonto Plateau**. **Hopi Point** provides a good view of **Granite Rapids**. Almost due north across the Canyon is **Shiva Temple**. From **Pima Point** one sees the ruins of **Hermit Camp**, an old **Santa Fe Railway** tourist shelter deep within the Canyon. **Hermit Creek** traces its narrow path through the desert, and beyond it is the **Lookout**, a massive formation with a cap of **Redwall Limestone**. Across the river is the monolith **Tower of Ra**, and to the east **Monument Creek** and the **Granite Rapids**. In the middle of the National Park is the small **Havasupai Reservation**, in a canyon rich in riparian vegetation and associated wildlife. **Havasu Creek** has waterfalls, cascades and pools which are favorite bathing spots. The **North Rim** or "**Arizona Strip**" slopes towards the Canyon, while the **South Rim** slopes away from it. The greater elevation gives the north side more precipitation, which has caused faster erosion. The North Rim's best-known feature is the **Kaibab Plateau**, and the visitor center of **Bright Angel Point** extends southeast from it. Across **Bright Angel Creek** are **Deva Temple**, **Brahman Temple** and **Zoroaster Temple**, and on the horizon the snowcapped **San Francisco Mountains**. The creek has cut all the way down a fault to the two-billion-year-old Precambian rocks. The **North Rim Forest** has spruce, fir and aspen, and lower down ponderosa and pinyon pines, junipers and Gambel oaks. Here the unique **Kaibab squirrel** lives, and a re-balanced ecosystem with deer, mountain lions, eagles and bobcats. **Point Imperial** is the easternmost viewpoint. To the left is **Marble Canyon**, and to the right the **Little Colorado**. In the foreground is **Mt. Hayden**, a pinnacle of white **Coconino Sandstone** resting on red **Hermit Shale**. The **Walhalla Plateau** is a peninsula of the **Kaibab Plateau**. From the promontory of **Cape Royal** one sees that the ponderosas have given way to more desert-like vegetation. Below are the **Unkar Rapids**. In the western part of the North Rim, at **Toroweap Point**, is **Vulcan's Throne**, a cinder cone 1.2 km. wide and 175 meters high, and **Lava Falls**, site of the Canyon's most dangerous rapids.

Montezuma Castle, *cliff dwellings inhabited by the* **Sinagua Indians** *in prehistoric times.*

MONTEZUMA CASTLE NATIONAL MONUMENT

Montezuma Castle National Monument is one of the Southwest's best-preserved cliff dwellings. Located in central Arizona about 80 miles north of Phoenix, it is called a castle because of its 5-story, 20-room structure, built in a cliff cave about 120 ft. above the valley floor. It was constructed by the **Sinagua Indians** about 1100 AD, and remains almost completely intact. The national monument, covering 1½ square miles, was established in 1906. These dwellings built in shallow caves in the recessed cliffs served as natural shelters from the elements, and caves with eastern or southern exposures had the advantage of being warm in the morning and cool in the evening. Many lay close to a spring, above a river valley with arable land. Perched high on canyon ledges, they were also inaccessible from above, approachable only by removable ladders or hand- and foot-holds

cut into the cliff faces, and thus were virtually impregnable to hostile outsiders. Part of the dramatic impact of this "apartment dwelling" derives from its sudden appearance high on the cliff as you approach it from the **Visitor Center**. Tourists may not enter the well-preserved structure, but signs and archeological and natural history displays, including a cutaway model, provide abundant information on the prehistoric settlement. Seven miles northeast of the castle is **Montezuma Well**, a limestone sink forming a small lake (470 feet across, 55 feet deep) ringed with large trees, which contributes 1½ million gallons of water a day to nearby **Beaver Creek** and the area's farms. The Indians who lived there centuries ago designed an irrigation system to divert the water to their fields, and sections of the ditches can still be seen, as well as ruins of their houses along the trails.

SEDONA

The city of **Sedona** sits at the southern extremity of **Oak Creek Canyon** in **Red Rock County**, 125 miles north of **Phoenix** and 27 miles south of **Flagstaff**, where the **Colorado Plateau** country gives way to the **Sonora Desert**. Prehistoric **Hohokam** and **Sinagua Indians** built sheltered communities in the Red Rock Canyon walls, but had already departed mysteriously before white settlers came in the late 1800s. Sedona was founded in 1902, named for **Sedona Schnebly**, wife of **Theodore Schebly**, the town's first postmaster. The abundant waters of Oak Creek permitted the little city to flourish through farming and tourism, and since the 1960s artists and writers have created a sizeable community, and opened many studios and galleries.

The natural beauty of the Sedona area is so overwhelming that New Age mystics claim it as one of the earth's major points of "vortex energy". The Colorado Plateau, which drops 2000 feet at the **Mogollon Rim** to the Sonora Desert, has been eroded into a seeming infinity of bizarre pinnacles, crested buttes and deep canyons in shades of pink, rose, beige, taupe, scarlet and amber. Oak Creek continues its eternal work of cliff-carving and nourishing the year-round bankside green plants and the spring-and-summer carpet of wild flowers. Beguiling rock formations bear such names as **The Lovers**, **Cathedral Rock** and **Courthouse Butte**, while trails lead to such destinations as **Pumphouse Wash** and **Devils Bridge**.

Although what first drew tourists to Red Rock Country was the gorgeous scenery, today they can also enjoy fiestas, festivals, art exhibits and Native American crafts shows. And there is every kind of accommodation, from campgrounds and bungalows to deluxe resorts with golf, tennis, heated swimming pools and bridal paths, as well as every kind of eating, from tacos to fine French cuisine and vintage wines.

The **Chapel of the Holy Cross**, a short distance above Sedona, was built in 1956 by **Marguerite Brunwig Staude**, a student of **Frank Lloyd Wright**. The imposing structure rises from a base of pinnacled rock between two natural peaks set against a mountain of red sandstone, with spires of white blossomed yuccas framing the scene; and its facade is formed by a simple but massive 90-ft. cross. Although the Chapel holds no regular services, visitors can stop to meditate inside this "man's church in Nature's cathedral".

The **Chapel of the Holy Cross**, "man's church in Nature's cathedral".

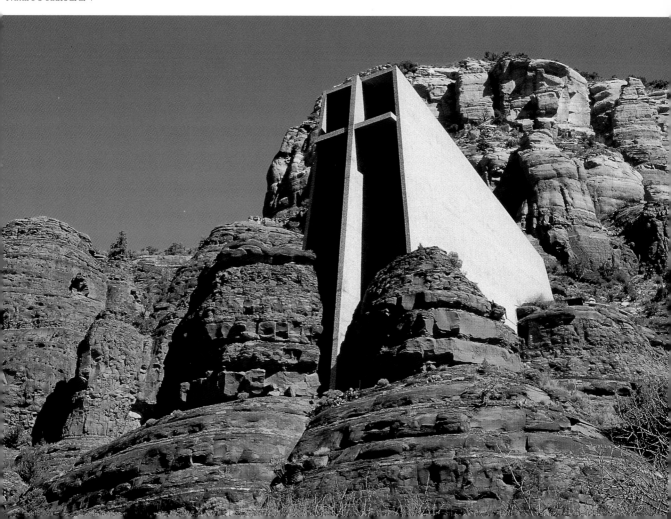

*Night view of **Phoenix**, legendary town of the **Old West**.*

PHOENIX

Phoenix, situated in the south central part of Arizona on the **Salt River**, is the state's capital and its largest city, with a population of 980,000. The **Hohokam Indians** inhabited the present site of Phoenix in 300 AD, and although they vanished more than 500 years ago traces of their culture have remained in the complex canal system of present-day Phoenix. The Hohokam culture has also been preserved in the city's museums and architecture. There are more than 23 **Indian reservations** in Arizona, home to more than 50,000 Native Americans from 17 different tribes. Modern Phoenix was founded on the banks of the Salt River in 1860, named by a settler who predicted that a great city would rise from the ancient Hohokam ruins, much as the mythical Phoenix rose from its own ashes.

The **Old West** is still alive in Phoenix in such places as **Frontier Town** or **Rawhide**, the latter an authentic recreation of an 1880s frontier town complete with barbershop, a replica of Arizona's first bank, and stagecoach and burro rides. **Heritage Square**, a city block of restored homes and museums preserved as a park, is highlighted by the elegant **Rosson House** built in 1895. The **Phoenix Zoo**, the largest private zoo in the nation, has more than 1,000 animals in habitat exhibits; of special interest is its **Arizona Exhibit**, with mammals, birds and reptiles of the Southwest. The **Desert Botanical Garden** is home to 10,000 fascinating desert plants, including cacti from as small as a thimble to as tall as a two-story house.

The Phoenix area has several Arabian horse farms and riding academies. Its scenic rivers are ideal for rafting, and **South Mountain Park** is ideal for hiking. There is **Arcosanti**, an ecological city of the future, and the **Hall of Flame Fire Museum** which houses the world's largest collection of fireighting equipment and memorabilia. The **Heard Museum** has an extensive collection of primitive and modern Native American art. The **Phoenix Art Museum** has a permanent collection of more than 18,000 artworks and costumes dating as far back as the 15th century. The **Scottsdale Center for the Arts** offers continuous exhibits of nationally touring art shows, exciting outdoor festivals, and film screenings. For music, theater and dance lovers there is the **Phoenix Symphony Orchestra**, the **Phoenix Little Theater**, the **Arizona Theater Company**, the **Arizona Opera**, and **Ballet Arizona**.

CASA GRANDE RUINS NATIONAL MONUMENT

The **Casa Grande Ruins National Monument**, just north of **Coolidge**, is Arizona's biggest and most mysterious prehistoric structure. The rectangular building is four stories high, and contains 11 rooms above an earthen platform, with wall thicknesses ranging from 4½ feet at the base to almost 2 feet near the top. About 3,000 tons of *caliche* mud were used to build it. The **Hohokam Indians**, the place's prehistoric inhabitants, had no stone and little wood available, and found this concrete-like hardpan a few feet below the soil, ground it and mixed it with water to make a kind of concrete they used for building-blocks, plaster, and sealing putty. Influenced by the great **Mexican civilizations**, the Hohokam had been farming the **Gila Valley** since around the time of Christ. Using stone-age tools, they dug hundreds of miles of irrigation canals and cultivated corn, beans, squash, cotton and tobacco. The Hohokam built Casa Grande around 1350 AD. Although this compound has the same layout as other Hohokam pueblos, with dwellings, work areas, courtyards and storage rooms, it is about four times as large. Archeologists are not certain what purpose Casa Grande served. One possiblity is that it was used for astronomical observations. Certain holes in the walls seem aligned with the sun at the summer solstice and with the moon during certain lunar phenomena, and one can speculate that, like Stonehenge, it functioned as a monumental calendar. Archeologists believe that the central part of the ruins was a community plaza or "ballacourt", where group activities, such as ballgames, took place. 200 yards north of the main compound is another compound with two platform mounds on top of which one-story structures were built, believed to have been the homes of the ruling class. By 1450 AD, for no apparent reason, the Hohokam abandoned Casa Grande together with all their other villages. The Jesuit priest **Eusebio Kino** charted the site in 1694, giving it the Spanish name for "big house".

Casa Grande Ruins National Monument, Arizona's biggest and most mysterious prehistoric structure.

Tucson, Arizona's second largest city.

El Presidio, a downtown area showing a mixture of Spanish, Mexican and American influences.

Old Courthouse, with its tile dome and its architecture combining Spanish, Moorish, and Southwest motifs.

TUCSON

Tucson, Arizona's second largest city, lies just 70 miles from the Mexican border, surrounded by the **Santa Catalina Mountains**. The original Indian settlement of *Stjukshon* - meaning "at the foot of dark mountain" (Sentinel Peak) - occupied the site when the Jesuit **Eusebio Kino** came in the late 17th century. The area became part of the U.S. Arizona territory with the **Gadsden Purchase** of 1853, and was the territorial capital until 1877. The arrival of the Southern Pacific Railroad in 1880 and the discovery of silver and copper brought prosperity.

Much of **old Tucson** still remains in its downtown specialty stores, art galleries and crafts shops. The **Tucson Museum of Art** (1975) has a collection of Spanish-Colonial, Mexican, Pre-Columbian, and Southwestern paintings and sculpture, plus a **Crafts Gallery**. Nearby are four historic adobe homes: the **Edward Nye Fish** house (1868), home of the **Tucson Museum of Art Library**; the **Hiram Sanford Stevens** home, now a restaurant; the **Romero House**, now part of the **Tucson Museum of Art School**; and **La Casa Cordova**, home of the **Mexican Heritage**

Museum. The **Old Town Artisans** shopping complex is housed in a group of 19th-century buildings. **El Adobe Patio** dates from territorial days. The downtown neighborhood of **El Presidio** offers a mixture of Spanish, Mexican and American influences, in the adobe **John C. Frémont House Museum**, in the old Spanish fortress drill field of **El Presidio Park**, and in the **Old County Courthouse** with its striking tile dome and eclectic architecture. Tucson's largest green space is **Reid Park**, hosting two 18-hole golf courses, **Hi Corbett Baseball Field**, and a small zoo featuring reproductions of the world's various climatic habitats. The **Flandrau Planetarium** features hands-on viewing of astronomical wonders. The **Arizona Heritage Center** narrates Arizona history from the Hohokams to 20th-century mining days. **Fort Lowell** army post is an ambient museum and public park offering exhibits on the Apache Indians. The beautifully landscaped **University of Arizona** campus offers several items of cultural interest. Its **Arizona State Museum** (1893) has one of the major collections of materials on prehistoric to contemporary southwest Indians. Its **Center for Creative**

Old Tucson Studios, where visitors can watch film production crews at work.

Mission San Xavier del Bac, the "Sistine Chapel of the United States".

Photography houses the archives of many great photographers, such as Ansel Adams, Edward Weston and Imogen Cunningham. A gallery at the northeast corner of the campus holds a fine collection of Renaissance to 20th-century art.

And its **Geological Building** displays fossil, mineral, and stone exhibits ranging from fine gemstones to a dinosaur footprint.

Old Tucson Studios is a year-round amusement park and the setting for many western movies and TV shows, where visitors can watch production crews at work shooting scenes. Producers of the movie *Arizona* built the town in 1939 as an almost full-scale replica of mid-19th-century Tucson, but instead of movie-set props they built it in the round of wood and adobe. Visitors can explore the extensive sets, ride on a replica of the **Butterfield Stagecoasch**, descend mine shafts in an ore wagon, tour the town in the open-chair cars of the **Old Tucson Railroad**, and even witness the daily gunfight on **Front Street**.

Jesuit Father **Eusebio Kino** established **Mission San Xavier del Bac** in 1700, naming it after his patron saint **Xavier**, and after **Bac** - meaning "where the water emerges" - a Papago village. "Anyone might have founded it," Kino later said, "but His whisper came to me." The original mission was destroyed, and the present church was built in 1797, one of the Southwest's finest examples of Spanish-Colonial Baroque architecture. Between the mission's two towers stands a marvelously **ornate stone portal** crowded with arches, scrolls, saints, seashells, and even a cat and a rat. The highly **decorated interior**, with its frescoed dome, statues, and stunningly carved polychrome *retablo*, though unusual for a mission church, was fully in keeping with the Jesuit aim of "attracting by its loveliness the unconverted" - in this case the Indians. Lacking the more precious building materials, the artisans painted the altar to imitate marble and the dados to imitate glazed tiles, and "chandeliers" were painted on the walls to augment the few real ones. Critics have called San Xavier del Bac the **"Sistine Chapel of the United States"** and "the most beautiful man-made object in America Deserta".

SAGUARO NAT'L MONUMENT AND PARK

The **Saguaro National Monument and Park**, east of Tucson, is dedicated to preserving the **saguaro cactus**, called **"The Sentinel of the Desert"**. The saguaro cactus, found only in the **Sonora Desert**, is the symbol of Arizona State. The saguaro has a huge water-storage capacity, necessary for survival through the long periods of drought, and resembles a pleated barrel that can expand like a bellows. It also helps the desert creatures to live, such as the woodpeckers and the tiny elf owls, which bore their homes within its fleshy stems. Its cream-colored blossoms appear in spring, and in midsummer its crimson egg-shaped fruit which the Indians eat and process into jam and wine. The plant develops very slowly, taking up to 25 years to grow 2 feet tall, though at maturity it can attain a height of 50 feet and weigh 10 tons, and in old age (150 years) it may have as many as 40 arms. A saguaro can live for 2 centuries.

Saguaro National Park, lying in two sections on either side of Tucson, was established in 1958 to safeguard the plant, whose young specimens were being crushed out by grazing cattle. The 21,000-acre **Tucson Mountain Unit** to the west has vast stands of saguaros, as well as **Signal Hill**, where the pre-historic **Hohokam Indians** left intriguing **petroglyphs**. Its **International Wildlife Museum** exhibits some 290 species of mammals, birds, and reptiles from around the world, and shows continuous documentary films. The Park's 62,000-acre eastern section, the **Rincon Mountain Unit**, displays saguaro cacti against the backdrop of **Rincon Peak** and **Mica Mountain**. It contains five different climate zones, and the **Cactus Forest Drive** in the Rincon Mountain foothills leads to picnic areas, a desert ecology trail, a nature trail, and wilderness hiking trails. The Hohokam petroglyphs atop Signal Hill depict human hands, arrows, concentric circles, and what may be suns. The images are layered with desert varnish, a natural dark patina of manganese and iron oxide that was easy to scratch through and furnished a contrasting background. Their meaning, as well as the precise epoch in which they were done, remain unknown, though archeologists speculate that they may have indicated water sources or served to mark the presence of certain clans in the area.

Saguaro cactus, "The Sentinel of the Desert".

Organ Pipe Cactus, the largest national monument in Arizona, dedicated to the preservation of this rare cactus.

ORGAN PIPE CACTUS NATIONAL MONUMENT

Organ Pipe Cactus National Monument, the largest national monument in Arizona, lies along the Mexican border on the western edge of the Papago Indian Reservation, a 516-square-mile stretch of desert-mountain land dedicated to the preservation of the rare cactus for which it is named. The **organ pipe cactus** resembles a saguaro with all its arms stemming straight up from its base, an effect reminiscent of church-organ pipes. The park contains 31 cactus types, including the rare **elephant tree**, as well as more than 270 bird species, plus bighorn sheep, kit foxes, bobcats, javelina, kangaroo rats and Gila monsters. The **Puerto Blanco Scenic Drive** leads to the oasis of **Quitobaquito**, where a natural spring feeds a pond ringed with cottonwoods, a place that slaked the thirst of travelers from Father Eusebio Kino to the fortyniners, as they journeyed on the *Camino del Diablo* or **"Devil's Highway"** across southern Arizona. Today Quitobaquito oasis is a reserve for coots, migrating ducks and other waterfowl. **Senita Basin** is populated by elephant trees, which are similar to organ pipe cactuses, with the added touch of gray "whiskers".

The **Ajo Mountain Drive** leads into the rugged foothills of **Mount Ajo** (4,808 feet), past majestic stands of organ pipe cactus. Hikers can take the **Estes Canyon-Bull Pasture Trail** through spectacular canyon and mountain scenery, ending up at a pasture formerly used by ranchers for cattle-grazing. The **Desert View Nature Trail** offers a fine panorama, and the **Victoria Mine Trail** leads to a former lead, silver and gold mine.

The monument's most beautiful sight, however, are the spring wildflowers nourished by the nine-inch annual rainfall: purple hedgehog cacti, yellow palo-verde blossoms, magenta owl's clover, blue lupines, apricot mallow, and desert marigolds.

Taos Pueblo: New Mexico's typical architectural style.

The **Pueblo Indians** had perfected a far-flung civilization when Europe was sunk in the Dark Ages

Steer skull with American flag, an emblem of the romantic frontier-day **Southwest**.

SANTA FE-TAOS AREA

Taos and **Santa Fe** constitute the two poles of an area sharing a common geography and history, remarkable for its natural splendor, its multi-layered cultures - **Indian**, **Hispanic** and **Anglo** - that go back to the ancient **Pueblo Civilization**, and as a center for artists and intellectuals. **Taos**, the smaller of the two with its 2,500 population, is located in north central New Mexico, at an altitude of 7,000 ft, while **Santa Fe**, the state capital, with its almost 50,000 inhabitants, lies 55 miles to the south, along the **Santa Fe River**, surrounded by the **Sangre de Cristo Mountains**.

The Santa Fe-Taos area's first inhabitants, some 12,000 years ago, were **Stone Age hunters** who by about 6,000 BC had developed a rudimentary agricultural culture, living in caves and other natural shelters. They learned to plant corn, beans and squash, weave baskets, make pottery, and eventually build circular pit-houses, which evolved into stone-and-adobe dwellings. From 900 to 1300 AD the great **Anasazi** civilization stretched from **Chaco Canyon** and **Mesa Verde** in the west and north, to **Frijoles Canyon** northwest of Santa Fe, centers dis-

tinguished by broad networks of roads and large, multi-storied stone complexes whose inhabitants elaborated sophisticated religions, irrigated far-flung farmlands and made precise astronomical calculations. Among scores of other adobe villages that sprang up along the Rio Grande during the Anasazi era, the large one of **Ogapoge** or **Kuapoge** occupied what is now Santa Fe. Around 1425 many of these settlements were abandoned, probably because of extended drought, though some, such as **Pecos Pueblo** and present-day Taos, survived, and the first Spaniards in New Mexico found some 150 pueblos still flourishing. The Spaniards, spurred by legendary reports of gold, arrived in 1539-40 from Mexico under **Francisco de Coronado**, and soon subjugated the pueblos. Finding no gold, the Spaniards turned to colonization. Their first permanent settlement, **San Gabriel** (1598) failed, and in 1617 **Pedro de Peralta** founded the **Santa Fe colony**. A long period of enslavement and forced religious conversion of the Indians followed, leading to the great **Indian revolt** of 1680, when the Spaniards were driven out for a 11-year period, until 1691,

*A row of old mailboxes and a mural: two common sights of the **Santa Fe scene**.*

*Santa Fe's **Institute of American Indian Arts Museum** exhibits over 50,000 Native American artifacts.*

*Modern **Santa Fe**, faithful to its multi-layered Indian, Hispanic and Anglo traditions.*

when they returned under **Diego de Vargas** to consolidate their rule. During the 18th century relative peace and harmony prevailed, the Indians were treated better, and their customs were more tolerated. From the early 1800s on there was an increasing influx into New Mexico of Anglo mountain men and explorers, especially after Mexico declared its independence from Spain in 1821. This strong Anglo presence in New Mexico favored the U.S. government's projects of territorial expansion, and with the **Mexican War** of 1846 all of New Mexico was annexed. From the very start the new Anglo ruling class of New Mexico systematically stole the Hispanics' land and suppressed the customs of the Indians, who were not even granted U.S. citizenship until the 1920s.

Lew Wallace, author of *Ben Hur* and New Mexico's Governor in the 1870s, was the first to popularize the beauty of the Santa Fe-Taos landscapes, and by the turn of the century the area had become a mecca for painters. The **Taos Society of Artists** was founded in the 1880s, and in the 1920s the **Santa Fe Art Colony**. Subsequently such artists and intellectuals as Mabel Dodge Luhan, Georgia O'Keeffe, Willa Cather, Mary Austin and D.H. Lawrence, and, in the 1940s and 50s, members of the Beat Generation, carried on this bohemian tradition.

The Santa Fe-Taos area abounds in historic sites. Santa Fe has: modern **Cristo Rey Church** with its 1760 stone *reredo*; the **Cross of the Martyrs Walkway**; **Loretto Chapel** (1878), first Gothic structure in the west; the **Oldest House** in the U.S.; 400-year-old **Santa Fe Plaza**; **San Miguel Chapel** (1625), oldest church in the U.S.; the **Santuario de Guadalupe** (1796); Romanesque-style **St. Francis Cathedral** (1886); picturesque **Sena Plaza**; the ancient Indian ruins at **Bandelier** and **Pecos National Monuments**; **San Jose Church** (1760); the **Santuario de Chimayo** (1816); the **Kit Carson Home**; the **Martinez Hacienda**; the many Indian, Hispanic and Anglo museums, such as the **Institute of American Indian Arts Museum**, the **Palace of the Governors**, and the **Museum of Fine Arts**; and the many pueblos, such as **San Felipe** and **Tesuque**. Taos has the **D.H. Lawrence Ranch**; **San Francisco de Asis Church** (1776); **Chaco Culture National Historical Park**; and the **Picuris** and **Taos pueblos**. Some of Santa Fe's many seasonal events are **Las Posadas**, **La Fiesta de Santa Fe**, and the **Rodeo de Santa Fe**. Some Taos festivals are the **Fiestas de Santiago y Santa Ana**, the **Arts Festival**, and the **Pueblo Powwow**.

The **Alamo**, site of the historic battle between Anglo-Texans and Mexicans, part of the saga of U. S. expansion to the Pacific.

SAN ANTONIO

San Antonio is the most "Mexican" U.S. city. With its 785,000 population, more than half of which are of Hispanic origin, it is the ninth largest American city and the third largest in Texas. The city's Hispanic splendor and mild winter climate, plus its proximity to lakes and to the Gulf Coast beaches, make it a great tourist attraction.

The city was founded as a **Spanish garrison** in 1718. Several missions, including the **Alamo**, were built around it, and settlers from the Canary Islands came in 1731. San Antonio played a prominent role in early Texas history, and the **Battle of the Alamo** (1836) was fought there during the American takeover of Texas. Its location at the start of the **Chisholm Trail** made San Antonio a major gathering point of cattle drives, and up to World War II it was the largest city in Texas.

San Antonio lies on the banks of the small jade-green **San Antonio River** which meanders under several bridges along the magnificent **Paseo del Rio** or **River Walk**. Stretching from the **King William District** to the **Municipal Auditorium**, the River Walk dates from the years 1939-41, and its sections of tranquil cobblestone walkways, lush green subtropical foliage, sidewalk cafés, exotic restaurants, boutiques, art galleries, nightclubs and hotels make it a paradise in the midst of the busy downtown district.

San Antonio is renowned as a city of festivals. The most important is la **Fiesta San Antonio** in mid-April. Two others are the **Fiesta Flambeau** with its nighttime torchlit parade, and the **Livestock Show and Rodeo** in February.

Adjacent to River Walk is picturesque **La Villita**, a city block resembling the original Spanish settlement of **Yuanaguana**. Stone walls surround the area's brick and tile paved streets and plazas; haciendas rise alongside adobe shops and galleries, together with early Victorian and natural cut limestone buildings, all beautifully planted with bananas and bougainvilleas. La Villita is a center of arts, crafts and entertainment. Of particular note is **Cos House** (1835), site of General Cos' surrender to the Anglo-Texans. La Villita is also the site of Fiesta San Antonio's **Night in Old San Antonio**, a multiethnic eating extravaganza.

San Antonio's best-known attraction is of course the **Alamo**. Established in 1718 as a Mission, the Alamo later became a fort, and was the place where the small Anglo-Texan garrison under William Travis fought against the troops of Santa Ana. All that remains of the original fort are the baroque-style church and part of the convent walls. Near the church is the **Long Barracks Museum**, with relics dating from the Republic of Texas.

During the 1968 **World's Fair** in San Antonio, known as **HemisFair**, many spectacular modern buildings were constructed, among which the **Tower of the Americas** with its 750-foot high antenna and glass-walled external elevators which rise to a 500-foot observation level and a revolving restaurant.

*The **Tower Life Building**, the city's first real skyscraper, in the heart of downtown San Antonio.*

*The **River Walk**, a paradise of cobblestone lanes, lush vegetation, shops and outdoor cafés in the midst of the busy downtown district.*

The **Space Needle** and **Downtown Seattle,** symbols of a thriving present-day metropolis that is yet the most livable U.S. city.

The 605-ft Space Needle was built for the **Century 21 Exposition** in 1962.

The **burial place of Chief Sealth,** near Suquamish

SEATTLE

Seattle, with half San Francisco's population and twice its land area, and with a lush pristine nature on all sides, is considered today the **most livable U.S. city**. To the west are **Puget Sound** and **Olympic National Park**, to the southwest **Mount St. Helens**, to the southeast **Mount Rainier**, to the east **Lakes Washington and Sammamish** and the **Cascades mountain range**.

The city was named after the friendly **Indian Chief Sealth**, and was founded in 1851-2, though Puget Sound had been explored by the **Spaniards** and by the **British** in the preceding centuries. Up to the 1880s Seattle was a **lumber town**, but the arrival of the railroads stimulated trade with Asia, and the **Yukon Gold Rush** crowned its economic growth. **Elliott Bay harbor** is both a **major Asia-oriented port** and the **chief gateway to Alaska**. Since the 1920s **Boeing Aircraft** has been the mainstay of the city's economy.

Seattle was originally hilly but in the late 1800s it was made flat through controlled water erosion; the eroded earth was used to raise the street levels, so that many ground floors became basements.

Seattle's most noticeable landmark is the **Space Needle**, built for the **1962 World's Fair**. The Fair site, now **Seattle Center**, also contains the **Coliseum** and the **Arena**, the **Bagley Wright Theater**, the **Fun Forest**, **Center House**, the **Pacific Science Center** and the **Opera House**.

The **Old Waterfront** hosts many unique shops and restaurants, the **Seattle Aquarium**, **Waterfront Park** and the old **Alaska Ferry Dock**. **Pioneer Square** is the center of an attractive shopping and restaurant area, and nearby **Pike Place Market** is full of seafood and other gourmet food stalls, as well as eating spots and gift shops. The huge **Kingdome** sports and exhibition arena can hold 80,000 people.

The **International District** is an area of trans-Pacific peoples, especially Chinese and Japanese, and is full of excellent restaurants. The **Chittenden Locks**, joining Puget Sound to Lakes Union and Washington, offer the spectacle of salmon climbing. The **Business District** boasts a variety of skyscrapers, from the 15-storey **Alaska Building** (1905) to the 730 foot high **Washington State Convention and Trade Center** (1988). **Northwest Indian arts and artifacts** can be seen at the **Thomas Burke Museum** and at the **Suquamish Museum** outside the city.

Tacoma: panorama from the Harbor.

Mt. Rainier, 14,410 ft high at its Columbia summit, called "Tahoma" by the Indians, first scaled by Civil War general Hazard Stevens in 1870.

Mt. St. Helens, once called the "ice cream cone in the sky", had been dormant for 123 years before it blew its top on March 10, 1980.

TACOMA
AND OTHER PLACES

Most of Washington's 4.5 million population occupies a 10-mile-wide corridor from the Canadian to the Oregon borders, with peaks in the **Seattle** and **Tacoma** areas. Tacoma, on Puget Sound, is the state's third largest city, with a population of 159,000. The city's major cultural attractions are the **Tacoma Art Museum**, with its exhibits of French and American paintings, and the **Washington State Historical Society Museum**, with its oriental and Native American exhibits; its main wilderness site is 500-acre **Point Defiance Park**, which includes a zoo and an aquarium, and the fairytale amusement area of **Never Never Land**. **Spokane** in the east, with its 177,000 population, is Washington's second largest city. Its major sites of interest are the **Eastern Washington State Historical Society**, the **Cheney Cowles Memorial Museum**, the **Museum of Native American Cultures** and the former **Expo '74** area, with its **Science Center**, **Japanese Garden**, **Canada Island**, and suspension bridge and skyride over **Spokane Falls**. **Bellingham** in the northwest has the **Whatcom Museum of History and Art**, and **Walla Walla** in the southeast has the **Whitman Mission National Historic Site**. In addition, there are many pioneer and Indian culture museums scattered throughout the state, such as **Fort Okanogan** and **Fort Simcoe**, and the **Toppenish Historical Museum of Indian Crafts** near Yakima.

WILDERNESS AREAS

Washington, "the **Evergreen State**", named after the nation's founding father, lies at the extreme northwest of the continental U.S., bounded on the north by Canada, on the east by Idaho, by Oregon on the south, and by **Puget Sound** and the Pacific Ocean on the west. Its capital is **Olympia**.
The state's 157-mile coastline actually expands to 3,026 miles because of **Puget Sound's** myriad of inlets and small islands. Puget Sound and the **Straits of Georgia** and of **Juan De Fuca** divide the **Olympic Mountain** peninsula from Canada's Vancouver Island. The Puget Sound lowland to the east passes into the **Cascade Range** whose highest peak is

*Two views of the Pacific Coast at **Olympic Nat'l Park**, which is listed among the 200 World Heritage Parks for its extreme contrasts of climate and geography; above, sunset at **La Push**.*

14,500-ft **Mount Rainier**. The glacier-sculpted Cascades include many dormant volcanos, the most famous **Mt. St. Helens** which literally blew its top in 1980. To the north are the **Okanogan Highlands**, and the foothills of the **Rockies** begin toward the Idaho border. The Puget Sound lowland and the triangular mountain-girded **Columbia Basin** are Washington's only extensive level zones. **San Juan Island**, covering 55 sq miles, is the largest of the archipelago which takes its name, and **Friday Harbor** is the capital of this island group. The **Columbia River** system drains all of eastern Washington, while lesser rivers, such as the **Skagit** and the **Snohomish**, drain the state's western area. **Lake Chelan**, east of the Cascade Range, is Washington's biggest natural lake, and **Grand Coulee Dam's Lake Roosevelt** is its biggest artificial one. Washington has two major climatic areas: a moist, temperate zone to the west, and a dry continental region to the east, which includes the **Palouse Country**, a treeless area of low hills whose loess soil, the most fertile in the world, is ideal for wheat-growing. Washington's abundant animal life includes bears, elks, deer, cougars, bobcats, marten, skunks, foxes, and coyotes, many wildfowl species, trout, salmon and shellfish - especially the tasty Dungeness crab.

Almost half of Washington's land area is devoted to recreation, with 3 national parks - **Olympic**, **Mount Rainier** and **North Cascades** - 9 national forests (among which **Mount Baker-Snoqualmie**, **Gifford Pinchot**, and **Olympic**), and 150 state parks, as well as many ski and beach resorts, and hunting and fishing facilities.

American Indians - including the **Chinook** in the west and the **Nez Percé** of the interior plateau - have lived in the Washington area for over 10,000 years. The Spanish and the English explored the coastal regions in the 16th-18th centuries, but overland exploration was begun only with the **Lewis and Clark Expedition** in 1805-06. Fur-trading was the primary industry until the first settlers came, during the 1830s, into the Puget Sound area. The **Columbia Territory** was established in 1853. Subsequently, the lumber, coal, mining, canning and agriculture industries flourished, especially with the arrival of the Northern Pacific and Great Northern Railroads. Statehood was granted in 1889.

Palouse Country, with its deep rich loess soil, is the world's best wheat-growing area.

Toppenish's Outdoor Mural Program sponsors a festival each year in which 15 artists must complete a wall-sized mural in a day.

Olympic Nat'l Park: Hoh Rain Forest, with its 140 annual inches of rain, keeps the 200-ft-tall conifers perpetually green.

San Juan Island, Friday Harbor, the island's county seat and commercial center, where half its population lives.

Jacksonville, in the Siskiyou foothills, is an old frontier town, and Oregon's first designated national historical landmark.

Coos Bay, Oregon's "Bay Area", with its beautiful beaches and scenic and historic state parks.

Oregon, "the **Beaver State**", lies along the Pacific Ocean coast, bordered by Washington on the north, Idaho on the east, and Nevada and California on the south. Its capital is **Salem**.

Oregon has seven geographic regions: the **Coast Range**; the southern **Klamath** or **Siskiyou Mountains** (highest point **Mount Ashland**); the populous **Willamette River Valley** west of the Coast Range; the **Cascade Range** (highest point **Mount Hood**) east of the Willamette valley; the **Deschutes-Umatilla Plateau**, Oregon's wheat belt, east of the Cascades; northeast of this plateau, the glacier-sculpted **Blue Mountain Region**, which includes **Snake River Canyon**; and lastly, in the southeast, the **High Lava Plains** and the **Basin and Range Province** (highest point **Steens Mountain**), also called the **Oregon Desert**. The **Columbia River** borders with Washington, draining 60% of Oregon's land. The lower Columbia River, together with its two main tributaries, the **Snake** and **Willamette rivers**, is the third largest in the U.S. **Klamath Lake** is the state's largest, and **Crater Lake** is the deepest in the U.S. With its extensive hardwood and Douglas fir forests, Oregon is America's leading lumber state. It abounds in deer, antelope, elk, and bear, game birds and waterfowl. Seals, sea lions and sea otters inhabit its coast, where whales are often sighted in season. The main cities of **Portland**, **Eugene**, **Salem**, **Corvallis**, **Springfield**, **Medford**, and **Astoria** contain 59% of the state's 3 million population. The state higher education system includes 7 institutions. Oregon is rich in recreational facilities, including **Crater Lake National Park**, 3 national monuments, 13 national forests, 242 state recreation areas, and various county parks.

Indians - including the **Chinook** and **Nez Percé** - came to Oregon at least 10,000 years ago. Although ships frequently touched the Oregon coast through the early 1800s, the first inland explorations were carried out by **Lewis and Clark** in 1805-06. Subsequently, intensive fur-trading began, and the first settlers arrived in the 1830s, mainly in the **Willamette Valley**. A territorial government was set up in 1843. After 1850 immigration increased, and in 1859 Oregon was admitted to the Union. In the 1870s the railroads arrived, stimulating the timber and other industries, and connecting Oregon's agriculture with eastern markets.

"The Rock", Alcatraz, in San Francisco Bay, originally a military prison, from 1933 to 1963 was the most famous U.S. maximum security prison; it is now part of the Golden Gate National Recreation Area.

The Golden Gate Bridge, chief symbol both of San Francisco and of all California.

SAN FRANCISCO

San Francisco, with its 43 hills and spectacular views, can justly be termed the **most beautiful bay city of the world**. Its mild climate, cosmopolitan population, graceful Victorian and modern architecture, and bustling commercial activity make it **the cultural and economic hub** of a vast geographical area stretching **from Alaska to Mexico** and **from the Western U.S. to Oceania and Asia**.

Lying at the tip of the **Bay Area peninsula**, San Francisco occupies a space roughly the size of Manhattan and has a **population of 800,000**. Like Manhattan, it is also the center of a 5-county metropolitan area comprising many millions of inhabitants. The Spanish, in 1776, established a fortress at the site of the present **Presidio military base**.

The territory passed to Mexico in 1821, and the first civilian settlement, named **Yerba Buena**, was founded in 1835. The **U.S.** took **possession** of it in 1846, during the Mexican War, and changed the name to San Francisco. The **Gold Rush of 1848** and the **1859 Comstock lode silver strike** greatly expanded the city's wealth and population, and with the construction of the railroads it became **the chief port of trade with the Orient**.

In the 1890's San Francisco was nicknamed "The City" and became a **haven for Bohemians**. The **1906 earthquake and fire** destroyed vast portions of San Francisco, though it was quickly rebuilt.

During World War II San Francisco was the center of war-related industries and of strategic operations in the Pacific. In the **50's and 60's** it became the **headquarters of the beat and the hippie generations**, and in the **70's and 80's** it established itself as the **financial center of the electronics industry**.

The city maintains various cultural institutions, includ-

ing the **Opera House**, **three museums** and the **California Academy of Sciences**.

Chief symbol, not only of San Francisco, but of all California, is the **Golden Gate Bridge**, which crosses the Golden Gate straits at the very mouth of the Bay, connecting San Francisco with beautiful lush **Marin County**.

Designed by engineer Joseph Strauss, and completed in 1937, this masterpiece of functional architecture also suggests a majestic work of art, a sculpture that is at once romantic and modern, with its single orange-red span suspended between the ocean fog and the sunlit bay - an emblem of enthusiastic discovery and rediscovery of a city which is itself a hymn to joy.

Mission Delores (the small building on the left), one of the network of 21 missions erected by the Spanish Franciscan monks in the late 18th century to convert the California Indians, is situated between San Francisco's gay **Castro Street** area and the Hispanic **Mission District**.

Though the architecture of the Mission is generally simple, its altar decorations are rich with original Spanish and Mexican baroque and rococo motifs.

At the heart of San Francisco's downtown district is **City Hall**, hub of the **Civic Center** complex, which was constructed shortly after the 1906 earthquake had destroyed the city's original civic buildings. Designed by architect Arthur Brown Jr., City Hall is an excellent example of the neo-classical Beaux Arts style, and its dome is actually taller than the U.S. Capitol Building's in Washington, D.C.

Further on toward the Bay is **Lombard Street**, called "the crookedest street in the world", and one of San Francisco's steepest.

Its redbrick pavement runs through hairpin turns and around beautifully landscaped islands all the way down **Russian Hill**, a chic district studded with elegant modern homes and traditionally inhabited by artists and intellectuals. Lombard Street commands some of the most spectacular views of the city.

The **Transamerica Pyramid**, seen in almost every film set in this hyper-photogenic city, ranks by now as one of San Francisco's most familiar landmarks, though traditionalist San Franciscans regard it with a certain disapproval. It is the city's chief skyscraper, built in the late '60s, along with

Mission Delores, *picturesque 18th-century Spanish mission.*

City Hall, *an almost century-old neo-classical structure with a dome taller than the U.S. Capitol Building's.*

Lombard Street *zigzags steeply down chic panoramic Russian Hill.*

Transamerica Pyramid, *San Francisco's chief skyscraper.*

Chinatown, *the largest Chinese community outside of China.*

A Cable Car, *relic of San Francisco's first mass transit system.*

Pier 39, *center of cruise lines, seafood places and popular amusement spots*

Victorian homes, *also called "Painted Ladies", date from the late 1800s, and are modelled on four styles: Queen Anne, Stick, Italianate, and Georgian. Owing to their particular beauty, they are among the San Francisco sights most admired by tourists.*

the many other modernistic high-rises of the downtown **Financial District.**

Just west of the Financial District is **Chinatown**, the oldest Chinese community in the U.S., and the largest outside of Asia, presently numbering nearly 80,000 inhabitants (roughly one-tenth of San Francisco's population) and constantly on the increase with the influx of immigrants from Hong Kong, Taiwan, and most recently from Vietnam. Chinatown's bustling streets, among the city's oldest, are a gaudy bazaar of restaurants, import and souvenir shops, exotic food stands and mysterious herbal medicine stores. Chinese immigration to San Francisco started in the mid-nineteenth century. By 1850 there were already 4,000 Chinese, mainly from Canton, and their numbers increased in the following decades with the Gold Rush and the construction of the Transcontinental Railroad. A spectacle not to miss is **Chinese New Year**, a week-long celebration falling between January and March, with its papier-maché floats, marching bands playing percussive Chinese

music, and a block-long weaving dragon. Other interesting Chinatown sites are the **Buddha's Universal Church**, the largest Buddhist Temple in the U.S., and the **Chinese Historical Society of America**. One of San Francisco's most popular symbols is the **Cable Car**. Recently designated an official national landmark, the cable car represents the city's first mechanized mass transit system, dating from the 1880's. The three surviving cable car lines, the **Powell-Hyde**, the **Powell-Mason**, and the **California**, run on constantly moving underground cables which are wound into the **Cable Car Barn and Museum** on Washington and Mason Streets.

Just a short hop from the elegant trade centers of the **Cannery** and **Ghirardelli Square** is **Pier 39**, which offers a lively carnival atmosphere with its tourist boutiques, outdoor snack stands, seafood restaurants, mini-amusement park and multi-media show "The San Francisco Experience". Anchored on its docks are the Blue and Gold Fleet, offering sightseeing cruises of the Bay.

Old Fisherman's Wharf, formerly a fishing fleet station, now the home of a fish market and of quaint seafood restaurants.

Wildlife, which thrive in the area's unspoiled territory.

Monterey, a mixture of Spanish colonial and Victorian architectures, and the setting of John Steinbeck's **Cannery Row.**

MONTEREY

The **Monterey Peninsula**, with its azure sea, shimmering sea life, white beaches, rocky cliffs, cypress trees, raucous birds and capricious sea animals, is the most gorgeous stretch of coastline in California. First made famous in the writings of John Steinbeck (above all in *Cannery Row*) and as a sojourn in the '50s of Henry Miller, Monterey became a haven of the '60s flower children, who found in its Edenic nature a perfect setting for their alternative life-styles. Bounded to the north by **Monterey Bay**, to the west by the **Pacific Ocean**, and to the south by **Carmel Bay**, the Monterey Peninsula has in fact retained large stretches of unspoiled territory over the 17-Mile Drive, the Del Monte Forest, down through the Point Lobos State Reserve and Big Sur. Monterey Bay was discovered in 1602 by Spanish explorer Sebastian Vizcaino, who named it after a viceroy of New Spain, the Count of Monte Rey. The area was settled in 1770, and became the capital of Alta California in 1774, under both Spanish and Mexican rule. In the town of Monterey, **Old Fisherman's Wharf**, used in the 19th century in the cattle hides and tallow trade, then in the whaling industry, and in the 20th by Oriental and Italian fishermen, and in the sardine fishing and canning industry, since the 1950s has served as a main tourist attraction, with its quaint fish market and seafood restaurants, and as a departure point for sports fishing cruises. **Old Monterey** boasts such sights as the Spanish colonial **Royal Presidio Chapel**, built in 1770; the typical 19th-century adobe structures of **Larkin House** and **Casa Soberanes**; **California's First Theater**, where 19th-century melodramas are still performed; the **Old Customs House,** dating from the Mexican period; the New-England-style **Colton Hall**, California's first public building, where, upon acquiring U.S. statehood, the Constitutional Convention was held in 1849; and, in the rear of the same building, the **Old Monterey Jail**. Steinbeck's characters relive in their original Cannery Row setting in the **Spirit of Monterey Wax Museum**, also the home of the **Paul Masson Wine Museum** and of the **Monterey Bay Aquarium**, built in the 1980s, with its breathtaking reconstructions of Pacific sea-life habitats. Near Fisherman's Wharf is the **Monterey Conference Center**, offering business people a variety of convenient meeting facilities.

Pacific Grove coastline, *containing some of the greatest natural splendors in the world.*

The **Lone Cypress**, *along* **17-Mile Drive**, *a typical feature of the rugged landscape.*

The town of Monterey's waterfront **Recreation Trail**, used by joggers and cyclists, leads to the Victorian-style town of **Pacific Grove Point**, whose shoreline park is carpeted with exotic pink-and-fuchsia **ice plants**. On the westernmost tip of the Monterey Peninsula is the **Point Pinos Lighthouse**, California's oldest working lighthouse, dating from 1855, and home of the **Pacific Grove Museum of Natural History**. The **17-Mile Drive**, originally part of the Mission Trail, encompasses much of the natural and man-made beauty of the southwestern Monterey Peninsula, starting at Pacific Grove and swinging along the coast down to exclusive **Pebble Beach** and **Carmel Bay**, where it loops back inland through pine-scented **Del Monte Forest**, in which inventor Samuel Morse established his **Botanical Reserve** to safeguard many of the forest's precious plants. **Carmel Mission,** founded in 1771 by Father Junipero Serra, was one of the seven missions the Franciscan Friar erected along the El Camino Real from San Diego to San Francisco, and a lovely example of the Spanish Baroque style. The town of **Carmel-by-the-sea**, founded at the turn-of-the-century as an artists' and writers' colony (the photographer Ansel Adams and the poet Robinson Jeffers lived there), is a conservationist's paradise, where billboards and neon signs are prohibited, and the automobile is discouraged, along its square mile of streets lined with low English-style cottages. The **Carmel River Valley**, celebrated by Steinbeck as an area of rare natural beauty full of wildlife, is composed of farms and vineyards against the backdrop of the **Santa Lucia mountains**, and its dry sunny climate favors the activities of golfing, hiking, tennis and especially horseback riding. **Point Lobos**, "the greatest meeting of land and water in the world", whose topography Robert Louis Stevenson used in *Treasure Island*, features startling, craggy rock formations worn away by the sea to form small islands, inlets, beach coves and outlying shoals inhabited by the sea lions, or *lobos marinos*, which gave the place its name. Finally, there is **Big Sur**, the 90-mile scenic coastline stretching from Carmel to the Hearst castle of San Simeon, where the Santa Lucia mountains meet the Pacific Ocean with breathtaking cliffs dropping as much as 1,000 feet to mainly rocky coast. "Rugged" is the word which best describes Big Sur, whose few tourists are mainly hikers and fishermen who come to admire its wilderness and wildlife.

Sonoma Valley, whose county seat Sonoma is home of the historic **Mission San Francisco Solano** *and was the site of the famous 1846* **Bear Flag Revolt** *which established the "Anglo-ruled" California Republic.*

THE WINE COUNTRY

Napa Valley and **Sonoma Valley** have made California wines famous and prized the world over, and have become as important as France's Burgundy or Italy's Chianti regions. The first vineyard in Sonoma was cultivated by the Jesuits as far back as the 1820s to produce wine for Mass, but wine production remained fairly local. The industry was also devastated by Prohibition, though after repeal it gradually revived. In 1934 the **California Wine Institute** was founded, and after World Ward II the University of California became a center for wine research. By the 1960s a true "culture of the vine" was spreading across the U.S., in friendly competition with the predominant "culture of the hop", and today a California Cabernet Sauvignon, a Merlot or a Chardonnay can equal or surpass its finest European counterpart. Many of Napa Valley's premier vineyards are concentrated in the area between the towns of **Napa** and **St. Helena**, where visitors may tour the wineries and participate in wine tastings. A pleasant alternative to driving is a **hot-air balloon** ride or else a ride on the **Wine Train**. A slow ascent

in a balloon is a fantastic way of viewing the countryside, composed of seemingly endless vineyards, rolling hills, small towns and cities. Stopoffs on the Wine Train include **Beringer**, **Christian Brothers**, **Charles Krug** and **Gallo**, all named after their original or present owners. Charles Krug first introduced wine-making to the Napa Valley in 1861, and his legacy is carried on by the **Peter Mondavi** family. At Beringer the outstanding landmark is the **Rhine House**, a wooden Gothic mansion the Beringer brothers constructed in 1883, modeling it on their home in Germany. The Beringers also built the estate's limestone caves for aging the wine in barrels. The Christian Brothers winery too was founded in the 1880s, before passing title to a Catholic educational order. Grafting onto California rootstock even saved the European wine industry from the terrible Phylloxera blight in the 1800s. St. Helena is in the vicinity of **Mount St. Helena**, an extinct volcano which gave rise to the hot springs of **Calistoga** located in the Napa Valley's northern perimeter. A relaxing way to spend a day in the

Napa Valley, many of whose premier vineyards are concentrated in the area between the towns of *Napa* and *St. Helena*.

Hot-air ballooning, a pleasant alternative to see Napa Valley.

area is to indulge in a mud bath, sauna or massage. The Napa and Sonoma Valleys have their literary memories. **Robert Louis Stevenson** lived for a period in Napa and immortalized Mount St. Helena as **Spyglass Hill** in *Treasure Island*. Sonoma County was the home of **Jack London** who poetically dubbed it "the Valley of the Moon" and built **"Wolf House"** (destroyed by arson) near **Glen Ellen**; a museum has been set up on the property, now the **Jack London State Park**. Before you take off to the county wineries and those in the adjacent **Russian River Valley**, the town of Sonoma merits a visit. Buildings of historic interest are clustered in and around the **Sonoma Plaza**, relics of the adobe-built **Mission San Francisco Solano**, founded in the 1820s as the very last of 21 Catholic outposts in California, then a part of Mexico. The old part of town was also the site of the famous 1846 **Bear Flag Revolt**, in which a small group of rebels led by John C. Fremont, in revolt against Mexico's attempt to expel all Americans from the territory, took possession of Sonoma and proclaimed an independent "California Republic".

Cathedral Rocks were named by the Ahwahneechee Indians POO-SEE-NA-CHUCKA (Mouseproof Rocks) because of the resemblance to their log food-storage caches.

El Capitan, massive, sheer-faced, 3000 foot-high guardian of the entrance to Yosemite Valley.

Half Dome, Yosemite's symbol, rises 4882 ft. at its eastern end.

Following pages: landscape of *Yosemite Valley.*

YOSEMITE NATIONAL PARK

Yosemite Valley and its surroundings were formed over hundreds of thousands of years ago as a result of uplifting in the earth's crust, glaciation and erosion. The first inhabitants of the Valley were the **Miwok Indians**, who lived there peacefully until the California Gold Rush, when they were relocated. In 1864, Abraham Lincoln signed an Act of Congress guaranteeing the preservation of Yosemite, but it was above all the efforts of conservationist John Muir that were responsible for getting the territory declared a National Park in 1890. Massive, sheer-faced, 3000 foot-high **El Capitan** guards the entrance to Yosemite Valley. Another first dramatic view is upon exiting from the **Wawona Tunnel** (Tunnel View), with El Capitan on the left, and **Bridalveil Fall** on the right, flanked by the **Leaning Tower** and by the **Cathedral Rocks**. At the far end of the valley are **Sentinel Rock, Half Dome** and **Cloud's Rest**. The base elevation of the U-shaped glacially scooped valley averages 4000 ft. above sea level, and the rims rise an average of 3000 ft. almost straight up. **Half Dome**, Yosemite's symbol, rises

4882 ft. at its eastern end and can be reached from Happy Isles. The view from its summit reaches to **Tenaya Canyon**, to many of the prominent peaks of the **Tuolumne** area, and to the lush green Yosemite Valley. On its face Half Dome has the lichen-formed impression of a beautiful woman which in Indian legend is called TIS-SA-ACK. The **Three Brothers**, a granite formation named for Chief Tenaya's three sons, ascends like church gables which owe their form to fractures in the rock that crisscrosses the Sierras. The topmost point, **Eagle Peak**, 3779 ft. high, is the tallest on the north rim. The 2000 ft.-high **Cathedral Rocks** are remembered by oldtimers as The Three Graces, and the Ahwahneechee Indians had named the spires POO-SEE-NA-CHUCKA (Mouseproof Rocks) because of the resemblance to their log food-storage caches. Watchtower-shaped **Sentinel Rock** looms 3073 ft. above the Valley; to its right is **Sentinel Creek** which flows down to the **Merced River**; behind **Sentinel Fall** is **Sentinel Dome** whose summit is 8122 ft. The **Merced River** runs seven miles through Yosemite Valley down a

steep gorge to **El Portal**, then 18 miles through the Merced River Canyon, ending at **Bagby Dam**. After the spring thaw the swollen river subsides to a lazy drift for rafters and floaters, to become in summer a literal playground. During fall and winter receding water leaves still pools that reflect mirror images of the surrounding valley walls. Portions of the river freeze, creating sheets of ice that become a canvas for the swirling water underneath. The various habitats inside the park provide nesting, perching and hunting sites for over 120 species of birds. Yosemite is also home to a variety of mammals, many of which live on the valley floor, such as mule deer, raccoons, skunks, rabbits, squirrels, chipmunks, foxes and coyotes, as well as the potentially dangerous cougars and black bears. Two buildings worthy of note are the quaint **Yosemite Chapel**, over 110 years old, and the luxurious **Ahwahnee Hotel**, opened in 1927 to receive the park's more influential visitors. **Yosemite Falls**, over 2,400 feet high, are the most spectacular water display in the Valley. Beside it is 1,500 high **Lost Arrow Rock**. One of the most beautiful hiking trails is the one to **Vernal** and **Nevada Falls** by way of **Mist Trail** to the top where you can relax by the **Emerald Pool**. **Bridalveil Fall**, dropping 620 feet, and **Ribbon Fall**, dropping 1,612 feet, can be seen from the valley floor. **Glacier Point** affords a breathtakingly panoramic view of the whole park,

overlooking a sheer 3,100 drop, and especially of its most dramatic landmark, Half Dome, which divides the Merced River drainage from the tributary drainage of **Tenaya Creek**. On Highway 41 is the historic **Wawona Hotel**, Yosemite's "Sleepy Hollow", situated on a grassy knoll above an 18-hole golf course, and neatly tucked on the bank of the Merced River in Wawona is the **Pioneer History Center** with authentic relics of Yosemite's past. Also on Highway 41 is the **Mariposa Grove of Big Trees**, a forest of sequoias, some of which are 3,000 years old, the largest living things on earth. Yosemite Park also contains a vast wilderness known as the **High Country**, sprawling over 1,170 square miles and including the entire watershed of the mighty Merced and Tuolumne Rivers. Rugged mountain peaks rise over 13,000 feet, and the highest slopes collect heavy winter snows which melt in summer to form crystal clear brooks and streams that collect into alpine lakes lying scattered like jewels at the head of tremendous granite gorges. **Tioga Pass**, bisecting Yosemite from the east side of the Sierra at an altitude of 9,941 feet, is usually open between mid-June and late October. This pass was used by Native Americans, and became a popular mining trail during the late 1800s. Entry into the park from this entrance gives the visitor a panoramic view with lesser known yet equally dynamic landscapes.

*The **Three Brothers** group: the steep walls of these granite blocks and their pointed tops are all elements shared in common with other rock formations in the Yosemite Valley, caused by deep tectonic activity which has affected the entire area.*

*The outstanding **Yosemite Falls** in the omonimous Park.*

*The corrugation of the landscape in **Death Valley** is due to volcanic activity. Besides dunes, Death Valley has numerous salt and alkali flats, colorful rock formations, desert plants, small animal life and footprints of prehistoric animals.*

DEATH VALLEY N.M.

Few places in the world have captured the imagination quite like the **Death Valley National Monument**. It is a geologist's living laboratory - as well as the hottest place on earth. Death Valley was formed millions of years ago. Volcanic activity caused mountains to rise, and the valley floor subsequently became a giant lake. Evaporation left behind the salt flats for which Death Valley has become famous, and the sand dunes seem to extend beyond the horizon. Summer temperatures hover around 120°F. Mineral deposits have colored the artists's palette, while the brown, eroded hills of **Zabriskie Point** furnished the setting for the 1970 Michelangelo Antonioni film. Not far away is the **Devil's Golf Course**, seemingly made to order out of pure salt. The panorama from **Dante's View** takes in **Badwater**, a saline pond with the distinction of being the lowest point (282 ft. below sea level) in the entire Western Hemisphere, a decided contrast to Death Valley's highest point, **Telescope Peak** (11,000 ft.).

*A giant **sequoia** can attain a life-span of several thousand years, a height of 275 feet and a trunk width of 20 feet.*

SEQUOIA NATIONAL PARK

Unjustly overlooked by many visitors are the **Sequoia** and **Kings Canyon National Parks**, neighboring enclaves of the *sequoia gigantea*, the Sierra Nevada sequoia tree. In contrast to its tall and slender cousin the coastal redwood (*sequoia sempervirens*), the sequoia has two outstanding characteristics: an exceptional longevity and an extremely wide trunk. Coastal redwoods generally attain an age of "only" several hundred years, while several-thousand-year-old sequoias are not uncommon.

The most spectacular sequoias are naturally in the Sequoia National Park's **Giant Forest**, home to the General Sherman Tree, a contender for the *Guinness World Book of Records* thanks to its height (275 ft.) and width (36 ft.).

Take the **Congress Trail** for a walking tour of the grove and admire other mighty sequoias such as the President Lincoln and the President McKinley trees. Confirming the fairytale-like setting is the abundance of fairytale-like place names. One is the **Crystal Cave**, nestled deep in solid rock, and overlaid with stalagmites and stalactites. The **Lost Grove** is where a number of trees with 15-to-20 ft. trunks are found, and the best view can be had from the granite **Moro Rock**. Finally, the **Sierra Trail** joins up with the **John Muir Trail** to lead to **Mount Whitney**, at 14,491 ft. the highest North American peak outside Alaska.

The **Kings Canyon Park** is not without its interesting sights. Sheer canyon walls drop down to the **Kings River**, originally *Rio de los Santos Reyes*, named by a Spanish expedition in 1805 in honor of the Three Kings in the New Testament.

The 267-ft. Grant Tree, along with the Robert E. Lee Tree, is located in **Grant Grove**, and the **Big Stump Area** is a vivid example of what environmentalists have fought so hard to avoid.

133

SANTA BARBARA

The Spanish called this area "the beloved land", and deservedly so, for **Santa Barbara** boasts a beautiful location between the sea and the **Santa Ynez Mountains**, a near-perfect climate, palm trees and even a **Yacht Harbor**. Spanish mission architecture completes the final touch on a Mediterranean-like setting. Santa Barbara was capital of the silent film industry, and today many movie stars have their homes in the hills of **Montecito** to the south. When much of Santa Barbara was leveled by the 1929 earthquake, city administrators decided to reconstruct everything in a Mediterranean style.

One outstanding result of this was the eclectic **Santa Barbara County Courthouse**, a cross between a 15th-century Tuscan villa, a Spanish mission church with neoclassical entrance, and a Moorish interior.

From the Courthouse one can go to the nearby **El Presidio de Santa Barbara State Historic Park**. Although the area was first sighted in 1542, it was not named until 1602, and not until 1782 was the military stronghold, **El Presidio**, built, most of it later destroyed in the 1812 earthquake. *El Cuartel*, the military barracks, and *La Caneda Adobe*, an officer's home, are the only original vestiges; everything else has been carefully reconstructed. Under Spanish and later Mexican rule the society life of Alta California all took place in Santa Barbara. The colonial era can be glimpsed at the nearby **Santa Barbara Historical Society Museum**, which conserves period clothing and artifacts.

The original **Mission Santa Barbara** was finished in 1786, but the 1812 earthquake completely razed it, and it was reconstructed in 1820 in a blend of Spanish Renaissance and Moorish styles. Called "the Queen of the missions", it displays unusual features in the façade's Ionic columns and twin bell towers.

Next door are the **Santa Barbara Museum of Natural History** and the **Santa Barbara Botanical Gardens**. The Museum has a vast collection of fossils, rocks and minerals, lithographs by the naturalist Audubon, as well as a planetarium and observatory; it also houses tools and ornaments of the local Chumash tribe, and a huge skeleton of a blue whale. The Botanical Gardens has beautiful lawns, flowers, trees and meadows, as well as cacti in a desert environment. The oaks, pines and other evergreens na-

Santa Barbara's strong Mediterranean influence is immediately visible in the **County Courthouse***.*

*Santa Barbara is the only **mission** in California with two identical bell towers.*

*The **Yacht Harbor** is a prominent feature of the waterfront.*

tive to the central Coast have been replaced by the palms and aromatic eucalyptus trees which have become a city trademark.

Cormorants, herons and other sea birds nest in the saltwater marsh and lagoon of the **Andree Clark Bird Refuge**. Pelicans, too, are often spotted at the **Stearns Wharf**, a historic site that has been in continuous operation since 1877. The pier is home to shops, restaurants and the occasional fisherman, and its **Sea Center** displays local marine life.

The **Santa Barbara Museum of Art** features pre-Christian sculptures, Egyptian art, French Impressionist and German Expressionist canvases, photography, American naif and Oriental art. Santa Barbara's wide sandy beaches are alluring, despite the eyesore of offshore oil rigs.

The **Scenic Drive** is a good way to tour Santa Barbara by car, and information can be obtained at the visitor center.

Driving inland, one is reminded that the **Central Coast** is still ranch country, whose heritage is celebrated in the **Old Fiesta Days**, held in August.

Malibu Pier, where you can relive the Beach Boys era.

The entrance to the *Santa Monica Pier*, home of *Palisades Park* with its beautiful carnival playground.

Santa Monica beach, where you can just walk, or else rent a bike or rollerskates and glide along the special cement lane.

MALIBU

Malibu, home of surfing and of the Beach Boys, has been described as a Beverly Hills by the sea. The land was originally owned by the Rindge family, who sold it during the Depression. A legacy of the past is the Rindge mansion, now called **Adamson House**, a Mediterranean-style abode with beamed ceilings, ceramic tiles and a carefully landscaped garden. On the hills above the sea is **Pepperdine University**, from whose modern campus visitors get a breathtaking view. Surfers ride the ocean waves all year round, and the visitor can join them on the many excellent beaches, whether just to soak up the sun or to go swimming, wind-surfing, scuba-diving, snorkeling, fishing and boating. Surfriders Beach, close to **Malibu Pier**, is still a perfect place to relive the Beach Boys era. Many bird species find the salt marsh and lagoon habitat of **Malibu Creek** congenial. **Zuma Beach** stretches for miles, and rocky **Topanga State Beach** offers the chance to tour **Topanga Canyon State Park**. Rock singers, the art crowd and New Age adherents were the original settlers here in the '60s and '70s, followed by big names in the entertainment industry.

SANTA MONICA

Equally charming, and a definitely pedestrian-friendly town, is nearby **Santa Monica**, located at the very beginning of the Pacific Coast Highway between the ocean and the mountains. Scenic **Palisades Park** runs along the cliffs overlooking the ocean. At its southern end is **Santa Monica Pier**, built in 1908 when a railway line linked it with Downtown L.A. Along the boardwalk is a beautiful carnival playground with a handcrafted carousel, as well as several fine seafood restaurants, and an open-air photo exhibit illustrating the town's history. Tourists can walk on the beach or rent a bike or rollerskates and glide along the special cement lane. In from the Park is the **Third Street Promenade**, full of lively street entertainment. At the southern tip of the Promenade starts the **Santa Monica Place Mall**, with its specialty shops and department stores. The whole urban area by the ocean offers an incredible variety of restaurants, pubs, cafés, hotels and movie-theaters. South of here is Main Street, stretching between Pico and Marine, with galleries, antique shops, fine restaurants, and murals decorating many of the walls.

LOS ANGELES

The site of **Los Angeles** was discovered in 1542 by Juan **Cabrillo**. The *Pueblo de Los Angeles*, founded in 1781, remained a small community of ranchers up to the cession of California to the United States, when the **Gold Rush** created a boom in cattle sales. Since then many other booms have turned L.A. into the thriving megalopolis it is today. Despite its "non-centrality" L.A. boasts a distinct **Downtown**. The city began in and around the **Old Plaza** and **Olvera Street**, afterwards pushing west to **Pershing Square**. Fear of earthquakes early prohibited skyscrapers, with the resulting horizontal spread along **Wilshire Boulevard** to the **Pacific**, though advanced construction techniques have permitted numerous high-rises to be built since the '50s. At Pershing Square there are the **International Jewelry Center**, and on nearby Olive Street the Art-Deco-style **Oviatt Building** and the **Biltmore Hotel**. On 5th street is the Los Angeles **Central Library** with its 1926 pyramid-tower **Goodhue Building**, and across on Flower Street the **Arco Towers and Center**, whose plaza houses Herbert Bazer's **Double Ascension** sculpture. Opposite is the futuristic **Westin Bonaventure Hotel**, and across 4th Street stands the **World Trade Center**. The pedestrian bridge over Flower Street leads to the plazas, gardens and skyscrapers of **Bunker Hill**, on whose southern part is the 74-story **First Interstate World Center**, and flanking it the **Gas Company Tower** and the **444 Plaza Building**. The Victorian-style **Crocker Center** exits onto **California Plaza** and the **Museum of Contemporary Art (MOCA)**.

From here one can explore some of L.A.'s ethnic and cultural diversity: the **Grand Central Market**, with its Mexican and Chinese food stalls, and the **Latino commercial district** on Broadway. L.A.'s **Civic Center** consists of the **Pacific Stock Exchange** on Beaudry Avenue, the **Music Center** on Grand, the **L.A. Times Building**, and **City Hall**. East on 1st Street is **Little Tokyo**, with its **Japanese-American Cultural and Community Center, National Museum** and **Village Plaza**. **Chinatown** has distinctive restaurants, pastry shops and produce markets, as well as a traditional gate at **Mandarin Plaza**. **El Pueblo Historic Park** is the city's original nucleus, and on cobblestoned Olvera Street **Ávila Adobe**, L.A.'s oldest house, and colorful stalls selling authentic Mexican products.

*City Hall Tower, built in the 1920s, L.A.'s first skyscraper, frequently used as a film location; the Los Angeles downtown skyline, with the **First Interstate World Center** at the middle; open-air clothes stall, showing Hispanic-style wares, on colorful **Olvera St**; pagoda-like structures at the entrance to **Japantown**.*

*The **Arco Center Plaza**, brightened by Herbert Bazer's stair-shaped sculpture "Double Ascension".*

Hollywood, home of America's Dream Factory.

Melrose Avenue, a novel shopping district, home of the hip and trendy.

HOLLYWOOD

Grauman's (now **Mann's**)**Chinese Theater** on Hollywood Boulevard, has been famous since the '20s as the chief showplace of film premieres, and in front of it are the hand and footprints left by many screen celebrities. Down from there are **Mann's Egyptian Theater**, Hollywood's first movie palace (1922), and the **El Capitan** with its Spanish baroque exterior and Art Deco interior. One block east of the Chinese Theater is Spoony Singh's **Hollywood Wax Museum**, a further celebration of the Dream Factory. Further on is the corner of **Hollywood and Vine**, famous for the stars who used to cross the intersection. Just north on Vine is the **Capitol Records Building**, shaped like a stack of records with a needle on top. On Santa Monica Boulevard is the **Hollywood Memorial Park Cemetery**, final resting place of such stars as Rudolph Valentino, Peter Lorre and Douglas Fairbanks. Further south on Melrose Avenue are the **Paramount Studios**, open weekdays to tourists. In the northern hills is **Hollywoodland**, location of the famous **Hollywood sign**. West of Hollywood runs **Mulholland Drive** with its scenic

Mann's Chinese Theater and its famous floor where countless screen celebrities have left their hand, foot and even hoof-prints.

panorama of the **Los Angeles Basin** and the **San Fernando Valley**. Southwest of Mann's Chinese Theater, via **Sunset Boulevard**, is **West Hollywood**. Immediately west of Crescent Heights is the legendary hotel **Chateau Marmont**. On Sunset starts the famous **Strip**, with its celebrity-frequented clubs, bistros and restaurants. On Third Street is the **Farmers Market** with its open-air fruit-and-vegetable stalls and its souvenir shops and varied restaurants. **Melrose Avenue**, in the heart of an Orthodox Jewish neighborhood, is a novel shopping district, home of the hip and trendy, from funky antique shops to sophisticated clothing and new-wave and high-tech equipment stores, all with fascinating shop and window displays. At the western end of Melrose is the **Pacific Design Center** or "Blue Whale", full of shops specializing in interior decoration. Nestled in the Hollywood foothills is the **Hollywood Bowl**, home of the **Los Angeles Philharmonic** and the **Hollywood Bowl Orchestras**. It hosts numerous classical, pop and rock festivals, among which the **Fourth of July Fireworks Family Picnic concert**, the traditional **Easter Sunrise Service**, and the **"Open House at the Bowl"** children's festival.

UNIVERSAL STUDIOS

On the hills between Hollywood and the San Fernando Valley, a few minutes from the intersection of Highland and Hollywood Boulevard, is one of L.A.'s biggest year-round attractions, the **Universal City Studios**. Universal is largest studio in the world, with 561 buildings sprawling over 420 acres of mountain terrain and valley. Founded in 1915, Universal in the '30s became famous for its thrillers and horror films (including the original *Frankenstein*), later for many of Alfred Hitchcock's films, and such recent blockbusters as *Jaws*, *E.T.*, *Conan the Barbarian* and *Jurassic Park*.

From the **Visitor Entertainment Center** tourists can take guided tours aboard brightly colored trams throughout the entire studio. The **Back to the Future Ride** takes you back to the Ice Age and forward to the year 2015. In the **Backdraft** "show" you are engulfed in a firestorm of special effects. You can participate in the **E.T. Adventure**, and actually live through an 8.3 tremor in the **Earthquake Ride**. An early show is **Kongfrontation**, where you

meet King Kong, and another is the **Jaws Ride**. Another interesting part is the "movie worlds" where you can pass from frontier town of **Six Points Texas** to a **European street** to a **Colonial street** and a **New York street**. In **The Magic of Alfred Hitchcock** you can find out the secrets of the *Psycho* shower scene, and in the **Wild, Wild West Stunt Show** you can enjoy amazing antics by expert stunt-people. **The Adventures of Conan** is a magic show of sword fights, lasers and fireballs, and **The Star Trek Adventure** takes you aboard the Starship Enterprise to explore unknown galaxies.

Children are charmed by **An American Tail Show**, based on the Universal cartoon, and enjoy the giant props of **Fievel's Playland**. Visitors can also witness actual production sessions of a movie and meet the stars.

Universal City has been called **"the Entertainment Capital of the Entertainment Capital"**, and is second in popularity only to Disneyland. The visitor can also stroll through the recently built **Universal City Walk**, a futuristic village full of restaurants, shops and street performers.

Universal Studios, the largest movie studio in the world, and one of L.A.'s biggest year-round attractions.

BEVERLY HILLS

Although not necessarily or strictly related to the world of movies, **Beverly Hills**, like Hollywood, contains a special resonance throughout the world, even for those who simply hear or say its name. This autonomous municipality, completely encircled by Los Angeles, has become synonymous with a luxurious life-style which is not just typical of motion-picture stars, though they can be described as its original "colonizers".

It was in 1919 that silent-screen stars Mary Pickford and Douglas Fairbanks moved to this area and built their famous estate, **Pickfair**, hence starting a migration of movie celebrities that has never stopped. Located immediately west of Hollywood, Beverly Hills is mostly flat, with its northern section occupying the foothills of the **Santa Monica mountain range**. In 1914, when it was crated, it contained only 675 registered voters. In he '20s it became a "boom town" and has now become a population of more than 35,000. The **Civic Center** and **City Hall**, built in 1932, are classic examples of the city's Spanish Renaissance architecture.

You might also want to drive around the residential area north of **Santa Monica Boulevard** and just enjoy the amazing variety of beautiful houses and mansions. An important stop is the recently renovated **Beverly Hills Hotel**, with its Polo Lounge, where exclusive wheeling and dealing within the entertainment business traditionally occurs.

Beverly Hills has an undeniable reputation as a "shopper's paradise". But even if you don' feel like shopping, you might simply enjoy strolling around the so-called **"Golden Triangle"** district, bordered by **Little Santa Monica**, **Crescent Drive** and **Wilshire Boulevard**.

You cannot miss **Rodeo Drive**, cutting through the center of the triangle and world-famous for its collection of glossy high-fashion boutiques.

A recent development is **Two Rodeo Drive**, probably one of the most expensive shopping complexes ever built - its original cost was $130 million. You can visit its exclusive boutiques and salons in a European-style setting of cobblestone streets, elegant steps and an Italianate piazza. If shopping for high-fashion clothes or jewelry is not your primary interest, do not forget that each avenue of the Golden Triangle abounds with exquisite art galleries, antique shops and quaint restaurants.

Beverly Hills, famous ever since the silent movie era as the home of the stars.

Disneyland Park, *"the happiest place on earth"*, *with 10 million visitors each year.*

DISNEYLAND® PARK

Disneyland Park, in the intent of its founder Walt Disney, was supposed to be "the happiest place on earth", and, judging by its incredible success, it appears to have become just that. In steady expansion since its inauguration in 1955, the enormous theme park ranks as the single top attraction in the state of California, with 10 million people visiting each year. There are seven theme lands in all. **Main Street, U.S.A.** is the starting point, a nostalgic homage to turn-of-the-century smalltown life. At the **Disneyland Opera House** one can enjoy *Great Moments with Mr. Lincoln*, featuring special audio effects and animation.The summer after sunset there is the **Main Street Electrical Parade**, followed by the **Fantasy in the Sky** fireworks display. **Fantasyland** revisits the films *Peter Pan* and *Snow White*, as well as *The Wind in the Willows* and *Alice in Wonderland*. Even the *Abominable Snowman* is on hand, waiting to meet people in the thrilling **Matterhorn Bobsled** ride. The *Jungle Cruise* and the *Indiana Jones Adventure* are among the chief entertainments of **Adventureland**, while the **New Orleans Square** recreates an authentic rough-and-tumble Creole atmosphere around the town's distinctive buildings.

145

SIX FLAGS

Competing with Disneyland is **Six Flags Magic Mountain**, another big popular attraction, in the green community of **Valencia**, some 28 miles north of Downtown L.A. Inaugurated in 1974, **Mountain**, with its ponds, lakes, waterfalls and trees, and over 100 attractions and rides, is now one of seven Six Flags theme parks located throughout the U.S. Among its greatest thrills are **Roaring Rapids**, a daredevil whitewater river rafting adventure, and the spine-tingling rollercoaster called **Viper**. New park amusements include the **High Sierra Territory**, where you can shoot on a raft down the new **Yosemite Sam Sierra Falls**, and, for children, **Bugs Bunny World**, an amusement park which takes its cue from the famous cartoon character. Magic Mountain has many cafeterias and snackbars, but the best eating place is the **Four Winds**, an oriental restaurant situated at the park's summit.

*The **Six Flags Magic Mountain** theme park, the main competitor of Disneyland, located in the green community of **Valencia**.*

*The **Harbor**, one of the world's finest, served the Yankee trader ships and the fishing boats of the 1800s, and became an important U.S. Naval base in World War II.*

__Casa del Prado__, destroyed in the 1968 earthquake, was rebuilt in 1971, incorporating much of its original statuary.

SAN DIEGO

San Diego, in the extreme southwest near the Mexican border, is the sixth largest U.S. city, with a population of over a million. Juan Cabrillo discovered San Diego Bay in 1542, and in 1769 Father Junipero Serra dedicated the first California mission there.

The U.S captured the town from Mexico in 1846. The waterfront's **Embarcadero Walkway** winds from B Street to Marina Park past restaurants, piers with cruise ships and tour boats, naval vessels, fish markets, hotels and shops, as well as the restored sailing ships of the **Maritime Museum**.

San Diego's **downtown district** has the **County Administration Building** (1938) and the **Santa Fe Depot** (1915), both in the Spanish-Colonial style; the **Gaslamp Quarter** (1970s), a National Historic District area; **Horton Plaza**, an immense 6-floor commercial and entertainment mall; **Seaport Village** (1980), a beautiful setting of boutiques and restaurants; and the **Convention Center** (1990) with its 100,000 square-foot top-deck covered with white sails. San Diego's urban jewel is **Balboa Park**, 1,400 acres of canyons and hillsides north of downtown, chosen as the site of the 1915 Panama-California Exposition, and decorated with fountains, patios and ornamental vegetation. **Cabrillo Bridge** (1914) leads into **El Prado**, an avenue lined with San Diego's major museums. The **Museum of Man** has exhibits on various Native American cultures.

The **Museum of Art** features works from the Spanish Baroque, Italian Renaissance, and the Flemish and Dutch schools, as well as a Sculpture Garden with works by Henry Moore. The **Timken Gallery** is home to a small collection of European masterpieces from the 14th to the 20th century. To the south is the **Plaza de Panama** (1915) with its **Spreckles Outdoor Organ Pavilion** boasting the world's largest outdoor organ. Across El Prado is the **Botanical Building** (1915) with its over 500 varieties of tropical and subtropical plants. Next-door is the **Natural History Museum** (1874), and across from it the **Reuben H. Fleet Space Theater and Science Center** (1973).

147

San Diego - Coronado Bay Bridge curving 2.2 miles across
San Diego Bay from downtown to Coronado.

West along El Prado is the **Casa de Balboa** (1914;
reconstructed 1978), home of the **Museum of San
Diego History**, the **Model Railroad Museum**, the
Museum of Photographic Arts, and the **Hall of
Champions**. At **Pan American Plaza** are the
Aerospace Hall of Fame and Museum, with over
fifty original or replica aircraft. North of Plaza de
Balboa is the **Spanish Village** (1934-35), an art
colony consisting of thirty-nine Spanish-Renaissance
style cottages grouped around a colorful courtyard.
The **San Diego Zoo** (1916) occupies 100 acres in the
north of Balboa Park, with the world's largest wild-
animal collection housed in various habitats.
North of downtown is **Presidio Park**, site of the first
Spanish fortress and Catholic mission in California,
and of the **Junipero Serra Museum** (1929), which
has exhibits on Native American and early colonial
history.
Old Town, a six-block area just north of downtown
originally settled by the Spanish in the early 1800s, is
an extensive pedestrian mall full of quaint restaurants
and boutiques. The **Plaza de las Armas** is a frequent
site of art shows, and some of California's oldest
adobe and log houses are found here, including the
Robinson-Rose House (1853), the Spanish hacienda
Casa de Bandini (1829), the **Mason Street School**
(1851), the **Seely Stables**, the **Black Hawk Smithy**

and **Stable**, the social and political center **Casa de
Estudillo** (1829), and San Diego's first cemetery **El
Campo Santo** (1850). Old Town's most popular attraction is the **Bazaar del Mundo** (1971), which hosts
frequent arts and crafts shows and Mexican festivals.
7.8-acre **Heritage Park** was created to preserve
many of San Diego's Victorian houses, including
Temple Beth Israel, the **Sherman-Gilbert House**
(1887), the **Bushyhead House** (1887), and the
Christian House (1889).
South of downtown, across San Diego Bay, is the
peninsula community of **Coronado**, with large
Victorian houses on quiet tree-lined streets, many
public parks, and miles of superb beaches. **Harbor**
and **Shelter Islands**, in San Diego harbor, are lined
with marinas, hotels and restaurants. North of San
Diego is **Mission Bay Aquatic Park**, with 4,600 acres
of resort facilities, plus **Sea World**, the world's
largest marine-life park. **Point Loma**, on the mouth of
San Diego Bay, is a place of exceptional natural
beauty, featuring the **Cabrillo National Monument**
(1913), a **Visitor Center**, the **Bayside Trail** for hikers, **Point Loma Lighthouse** (1854), and the **Whale
Overlook**. North of Mission Beach is the coastal
community of **La Jolla**, "the Jewel of the Pacific", with
its seven miles of spectacular coastline, including
some of the best surfing beaches in San Diego.

LAS VEGAS

The once tiny village of **Las Vegas** first attracted California-bound travelers during the Gold Rush. The town became part of **Nevada State** in 1864, and was incorporated in 1905. Gambling was legalized in Nevada in 1931, and the population has been growing rapidly ever since. Las Vegas's gambling and entertainment industry attracts over 13 million visitors a year from all over the world. Its 320-day annual average of sunshine, plus its many scenic wonders and dazzling nightlife, make it irresistible.

Visitors are bowled over by the gaudy neon displays of hotels and casinos on the **"Las Vegas Strip"**, such mythic spots as **Caesar's Palace** with its gleaming classic statuary, the **Flamingo Hilton** with the largest swimming pool in Nevada, the **Barbary Coast** with its colorful entrance, the **Tropicana Hotel** with its Hawaiian motifs, **Bob Stupak's Vegas World Hotel-Casino** displaying the world's largest jackpot, **Bally's Grand Hotel** with the largest casino and shopping arcade of any hotel in the city, the **Stardust Hotel and Casino** with its magnificent 4,000-lightbulb display, the **Circus Hotel and Casino** with its circus acts, the famous **Copa Room**, the **Sahara Hotel** with its 20-acre complex, the **Showboat Hotel, Casino and Bowling Center** with its 106 championship lanes, the **Las Vegas Hilton**, largest resort and convention complex in the world, the **Hotel-Casino** with the lifelike Paddle-Wheel mural on its facade, and the **Lady Luck Casino & Hotel** with its nightly gaming tournaments. The **Las Vegas Casino Center**, where the city originated, at night seems illuminated to daylight by the rush of glittering neon displays, some of them so unusual they are considered contemporary works of art. Las Vegas has more stars and stage shows each night than any other city on earth, which is why it's called **"the Entertainment Capital of the World"**. The city also has many fine shops, often within the shopping malls of big hotels.

Las Vegas has many year-round golf courses, tennis courts, health clubs, jogging and bicycle trails, horseback riding facilities and arenas, archery ranges, trap and skeet ranges, and even bird and game hunting. For outside excursions, Las Vegas is within easy reach of the ski resort of **Lee Canyon**, **Hoover Dam**, **Lake Mead**, the **Valley of Fire State Park** and **Red Rock Canyon**.

Las Vegas, the world's gambling and entertainment capital. Here on view are **The Mirage**, **The Excalibur**, and the entrance to **Caesar's Palace**.

Oahu, third largest Hawaiian Island, whose main communities are *Honolulu*, *Kailua*, *Kaneohe*, *Wahiawa*, and *Waipahu*.

HONOLULU

Honolulu, Hawaii's capital and largest city, lies on the southeast coast of the island of **Oahu**, and with its population of 365,000 is a business and financial center for the Pacific. In 1794 the British explorer **Capt. William Brown** became the first European to enter Honolulu harbor, and Western missionaries arrived in 1820. Honolulu was named the permanent capital of the Hawaiian kingdom in 1845 and remained the capital through annexation to the United States in 1898 and statehood in 1959. The U.S. Naval Base at **Pearl Harbor**, to the west, was bombed by the Japanese on Dec. 7, 1941. Honolulu was a staging area for U.S. forces during World War II and the Korean and Vietnam wars.

Honolulu is among the most popular U.S. vacation spots, attracting more than 3 million visitors annually. It boasts a wealth of natural splendors. The most famous is the beach at **Waikiki**; the word means "springwater" since at one time it was swampland bathed by mountain springs today completely covered by asphalt and mega tourist hotels. The **Koolau Mountains'** nine-mile stretch of sheer cliffs opens on solitary gullies, small green valleys and crystal clear cascades. The windswept **Nuuanu Pali Lookout**, long considered Oahu's main attraction, offers staggering 360-degree panoramas of the entire island. **Diamond Head**, the most famous of Oahu's three extinct volcano craters, can actually be visited in its interior.

Honolulu is ethnically mixed: one-third Caucasian, one-third of Japanese origin, and the rest of Hawaiian, Chinese, and Filipino descent. The city is a center for the study of Pacific cultures. The **Bishop Museum** (1889) houses the world's largest collection of Hawaian and Polynesian artifacts. Then there are the **Honolulu Academy of Arts** (1926), the **University of Hawaii** (1907), and **Iolani Palace** (1882), once the home of the Hawaiian monarchs. The University's **East-West Center** (1960), founded to promote mutual understanding among the peoples of Asia, the Pacific and the U.S., hosts numerous monuments of the Orient, among which the Thai Pavilion donated by King Bhumibol Adulyadej in 1967. **Oahu**, the third largest of the Hawaiian Islands, has a population of 740,000. It became the seat of the royal government in the middle of the 19th century. Its main communities, after Honolulu, are **Kailua, Kaneohe, Wahiawa**, and **Waipahu**.

*Denali National Park: Wonder Lake, a favorite site for tent campers. The park boasts Alaska's highest peak, 20,320-ft **Mt. McKinley**.*

Anchorage is a modern though inhabitant-friendly city, with more than 70 miles of bike paths that lead through pleasant streets all over town.

ANCHORAGE

Anchorage, the "Los Angeles" of Alaska, with its 173,000 inhabitants, is the state's most populous and most sprawling city. Located at the head of **Cook Inlet**, the **Anchorage Bowl** forms a wide triangular plain with two long bays, the **Knit Arm** and the **Turnagain Arm**.

The **Chugachimiut Eskimos** and the **Tanaina Indians** lived in the Anchorage area from about 4,000 BC. **Captain James Cook** was the first European to explore the region in 1778. The city was founded in 1914 as a construction base for the **Alaska Railroad**, and developed as a railroad town for the coal, gold, and fishing industries. In World War II it became an important transportation and defense center. With the discovery of offshore oil, subsequent to the disastrous **1964 earthquake**, Anchorage attracted much new immigration, a factor which hastened its reconstruction and expansion.

Anchorage is a people-friendly city, boasting 70 miles of bike-paths, a good public transporatation system called the **"People Mover"**, two university campuses, a zoo, a historical and fine arts museum, and a symphony orchestra. It is also a scenically beautiful city, with the mighty tides from the northwest and southwest creating startling visual effects of patterned wetland and tidal bores, enhanced by the encircling mountains - the **Chugah** to the east, the **Talkeetnas** to the north, and the great **Aleutian Range** to the south. Anchorage also enjoys one of Alaska's most moderate climates. Anchorage really excels in its outdoor activities. Right in and around the city you can go rafting (on **Campbell Creek** in the heart of town), biking through pleasant streets, bird-watching on urban lakes and in publicly protected marshlands, and even cross-country skiing in the municipal parks. **Chugach Mountain State Park** just a few miles away offers hiking, backpacking, rock climbing, and cross-country skiing, while **Kenai National Wildlife Refuge** and **Prince William Sound** to the south offer canoeing, kayaking and sailing. For downhill skiing there is nearby **Alyeska**, as well as **Hatcher Pass** to the north. Anchorage's two great annual events are the February **Fur Rendezvous** ("Rondy") with its fur auction, and world championship sled-dog races and dog weight pull; and the March **Iditarod Race**, in which dog teams start from Anchorage on a 1,000-mile pull to Iditarod.

Two views of **Portage Glacier**, *whose 6-mile expanse reaches into* **Portage Lake**.

The **Virgin Islands**, seven main islands and over ninety islets and cays lying east of Puerto Rico in the Caribbean, cover an area of 192 square miles. The U.S. part, with a population of 102,000, includes **Saint Thomas**, **Saint Croix**, **Saint John**, and about 50 islets. **Charlotte Amalie** on Saint Thomas is its capital. Most Virgin Islanders have descended from the slaves who worked colonial plantations. The islands live mainly on tourism, though agriculture, as well as oil and bauxite production, are also important items in their economy.

Christopher Columbus landed at **Saint Croix** in 1493. The British took control of their presently-owned islands in 1666, the same year the Danes occupied Saint Thomas. In 1684 the Danes also took over Saint John, and purchased Saint Croix from the French in 1733. The U.S. purchased its islands from Denmark in 1917, owing to their strategic position on the route to the Panama Canal.

Some important sites on **Saint Thomas** are: *the Danish historic center of Charlotte Amalie; French town; the West India Company dock; Bluebeard's and*

Bluebeard's Castle, *atop Frederiksberg hill, thought to have once been the hole-up of the terrible pirate Bluebeard.*

St. Thomas Harbor, *a free port since 1724, its warehouses along Dronningens Gade bursting with tax-free luxury goods.*

St. John, **Trunk Bay**, *one of the most beautiful beaches of the island's reef-ringed northwest shore.*

St. Croix, **Fort Christianvaern**, *seen from the harbor.*

Blackbeard's Castles; Fort Christian (1671); Frederick Lutheran Church (1793); the Moravian Memorial Church (1844); Crown House (1750); Mark St. Thomas Hotel (1785); the once slave market of Dronningens Gade; Magens Bay, with Drake's Seat; Coral World Marine Park (1977); and nearby Coki Beach.

St. John, site of a famous slave rebellion in 1733, is the least populated and commercially developed island, 74% of it comprising the *Virgin Islands National Park.* Its main points of interest are: *Cruz Bay (1735);* the beautiful *Hawksnest, Trunk* and *Cinnamon Bays* within the Park; and the ex-slave market harbor of *Coral Bay.* **St. Croix**, once home of the **Arawak** and the fierce **Carib Indians**, is the largest of the islands and the most geographically diverse, with mountains and a rain forest in the north and desert grassland in the south. Its major sites are: *Fort Christianvaern (1749); Government House, (1742), the Steeple Building (1753); the Columbus Landing Site;* the town of *Frederiksted (1760); the St. George Village Botanical Gardens* with its 800 tropical plant species; and the *Estate Whim Plantation Museum.*

El Morro, with its lush tropical garden, *Casa Rosada* and *Casa Blanca Museum*.

Piñones, a scenic area of desert beaches, the *Luquillo Mountains*, and *"El Yunque"*, the only U.S. tropical rain forest.

Condado Lagoon, between San Juan Bay and the Atlantic, a perfect place for birdwathching, jogging and all kinds of water sports.

Puerto Rico, a U.S. commonwealth island whose capital is **San Juan**, lies east of the Dominican Republic and west of the Virgin Islands, at the northern rim of the Caribbean Sea. Its 3,435-square-mile area has a population of 3.5 million. The commonwealth also comprises several smaller offshore islands, such as **Culebra**, **Mona**, and **Vieques**.

Almost three-quarters of Puerto Rico is hilly or mountainous, the **Cordillera Central** and the **Sierra de Cayey** forming a backbone of ridges from west to east across the island, ringed by a narrow coastal plain. The island has few lakes or rivers, its soils are mostly unsuited for farming, and the deep waters surrounding it yield little fish, factors which in the past resulted in widespread poverty and emigration; however, in recent times its tropical climate and fine beaches have made it a mecca for tourism. **Columbus** discovered Puerto Rico - called by the Indians **Borinquén** - on his second trip to the New World, in 1493, and named it **San Juan Bautista**. In 1508 **Ponce De Leon** with 50 followers subdued the 30,000 Taino Indians, founded a settlement at **Caparra**, and gave the island its present name. By 1582 the Indians had virtually all died off. Meanwhile the Spaniards introduced the cultivation of sugarcane and began importing black slaves. The United States annexed Puerto Rico at the end of the **Spanish-American War**, and Puerto Ricans gained U.S. citizenship in 1917. **"Operation Bootstrap"**, a government plan to assist private enterprise in order to develop the island's economy, was undertaken in 1948, and the **Commonwealth of Puerto Rico** was established in 1952 under the island's first governor, **Luis Munoz Marin**. San Juan is full of Spanish-colonial architecture, including: elegant **Paseo de la Princesa**; the late-18th-century *muralla* or city wall; **La Fortaleza**, the oldest governor's mansion still in use in the western hemisphere; the estate of **El Morro** with its **Casa Rosada** (1812) and its **Casa Blanca Museum** of 16th-17th-century life; the Spanish baroque churches of **San José** and **San Juan**, and the small **Capilla de Cristo**; the **Pablo Casals Museum**; and the **Centro Nacional de Artes Populares y Artesanías**. **Loísa** is ideal for surfing. **Fajardo** is a major boating and sailing center, and boasts the **Las Cabezas de San Juan Nature Reserve**. The **Culebra National Wildlife Refuge** comprises areas of Culebra itself and 23 offshore islands.

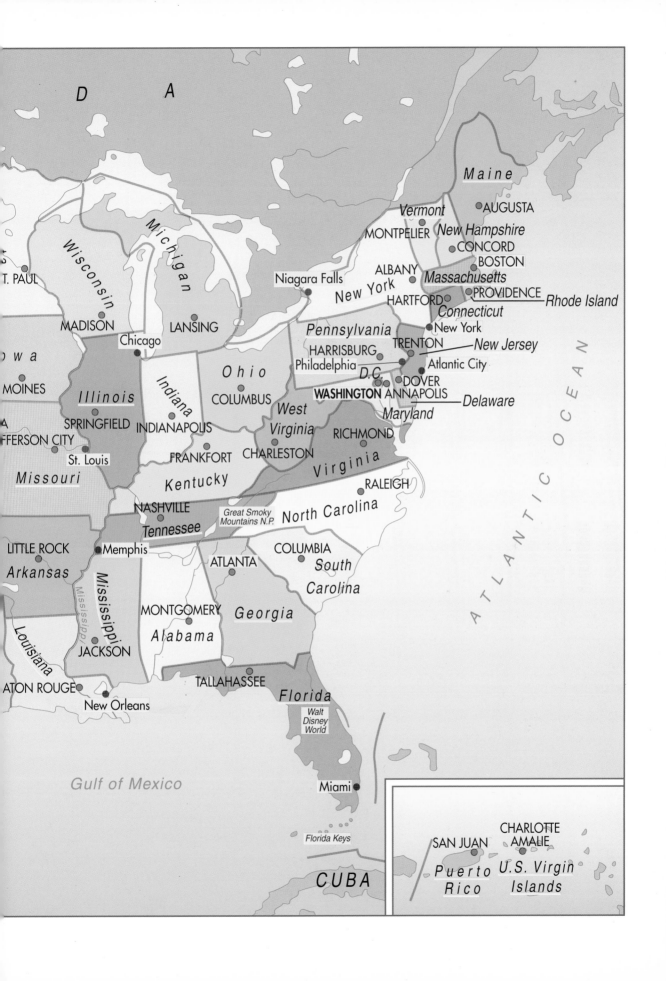

D   A

Maine

Michigan

Wisconsin

Vermont   • AUGUSTA
MONTPELIER   New Hampshire
                • CONCORD
ALBANY   • BOSTON
Niagara Falls   New York   Massachusetts
T. PAUL   New York   • PROVIDENCE
                            HARTFORD   Rhode Island
MADISON   LANSING   Connecticut
Chicago   Pennsylvania   New York
I o w a   HARRISBURG   TRENTON   New Jersey
MOINES   Philadelphia   Atlantic City
         Illinois   Indiana   O h i o   D.C.   DOVER
FFERSON CITY   SPRINGFIELD   COLUMBUS   WASHINGTON ANNAPOLIS   Delaware
         INDIANAPOLIS   West   Maryland
St. Louis   FRANKFORT   Virginia   RICHMOND
Missouri   Kentucky   CHARLESTON   V i r g i n i a

                                        RALEIGH
LITTLE ROCK   NASHVILLE   Great Smoky   North Carolina
Arkansas   Memphis   Tennessee   Mountains N.P.

                    COLUMBIA
         Mississippi   ATLANTA   South
                                  Carolina
         MONTGOMERY   Georgia
Louisiana   Alabama
ATON ROUGE   JACKSON
         New Orleans   TALLAHASSEE   Florida
                                      Walt
Gulf of Mexico   Disney
                                      World
                    Miami

                    Florida Keys

CUBA

A T L A N T I C   O C E A N

CHARLOTTE
AMALIE
SAN JUAN
Puerto   U.S. Virgin
Rico   Islands

INDEX

America also has its temporal dimensions.................3
A brief human history of America.............................5

ALASKA...152
Anchorage..152
ARIZONA...82
Casa Grande Ruins National Monument............89
Grand Canyon National Park..............................82
Montezuma Castle National Monument.............86
Organ Pipe Cactus National Monument.............97
Phoenix...88
Saguaro National Monument.............................94
Sedona..87
Tucson..90
CALIFORNIA..114
Beverly Hills...143
Death Valley National Monument.......................132
Disneyland Park...145
Hollywood...140
Los Angeles..139
Malibu...136
Monterey...120
San Diego...147
San Francisco...114
Santa Barbara..134
Santa Monica...136
Sequoia National Park...133
Six Flags...146
The Wine Country..124
Universal Studios...142
Yosemite National Park.......................................126
COLORADO...61
Colorado Plateau...61
Mesa Verde National Park..................................63
DISTRICT OF COLUMBIA...................................31
Washington, D.C...31
FLORIDA...36
Miami..36
The Florida Keys..40
GEORGIA..34
Atlanta..34
HAWAII...150
Honolulu...150
ILLINOIS...56
Chicago...56
LOUISIANA...46

New Orleans...46
MAINE..10
MASSACHUSETTS...14
Boston...14
MISSISSIPPI..42
Mississippi River..42
MISSOURI..52
St. Louis..52
NEVADA...149
Las Vegas...149
NEW JERSEY...25
Atlantic City...25
NEW MEXICO...98
Santa Fe - Taos Area...98
NEW YORK...18
New York City...21
Niagara Falls..18
OREGON..112
PENNSYLVANIA...26
Philadelphia..26
PUERTO RICO...156
SOUTH DAKOTA..60
Mt. Rushmore..60
TENNESSEE..50
Great Smoky Mountains Nat'l Park....................51
Memphis...50
TEXAS...102
San Antonio..102
U.S. VIRGIN ISLANDS......................................154
UTAH...70
Arches National Park...72
Bryce Canyon National Park...............................79
Canyonlands National Park.................................74
Capitol Reef National Park..................................78
Lake Powell..76
Monument Valley...75
Salt Lake City...70
Zion National Park...80
VERMONT..12
WASHINGTON...104
Seattle..104
Tacoma and other places....................................106
Wilderness Areas...106
WYOMING..64
Grand Teton National Park..................................69
Yellowstone National Park..................................64